putin's legacy

Russian Policy and the New Arms Race

ISBN: 1-4392-5589-X
ISBN-13: 9781439255896

"The misery that is now upon us is but the passing of greed, the bitterness of men who fear the way of human progress. The hate of men will pass, and dictators die, and the power they took from the people, will return to the people, and so long as men die liberty will never perish..."

Chaplin, in The Great Dictator (1940)

In Memorium

Piers Merchant (1952 – 2009)

Journalist, Parliamentarian, and Raconteur.

about the author

Gary Cartwright is a political scientist specialising in Energy and Environmental policy. He has extensive experience of working within the EU institutions in Brussels and Strasbourg in a number of policy areas. His main interest is in EU - Russia relations; he is a keen advocate of a common European energy policy, and has been widely published on this issue. He has ghost written articles and publications on subjects as diverse as the Lisbon Treaty and the Common Fisheries Policy.

Prior to his move to Brussels, Gary worked in education, and also lobbied on Veteran's affairs. An ex-serviceman himself, he was heavily involved in the successful campaign for the appointment of a Minister for Veteran's Affairs in the UK parliament. He is also very proud to have played a small part in the campaign for recognition, and compensation, for former Far East Prisoners of War. In 2004 he was campaign manager for Frank Maloney, the well-known boxing promoter and manager of world heavyweight champion Lennox Lewis, when he ran for the office of Mayor of London.

He is an accredited journalist, and is consulting editor of the Brussels based journal EU Reporter. (www.eureporter.co.uk).

His website, which covers EU-Russia relations, and examines Russian environmental issues, can be found at www.cartwright.eu.com

contents

introduction

In March 2006, an extraordinary meeting took place at the Victory Services Club in central London. I had received some interesting information from an acquaintance, Vladimir Bukovsky, a prominent Russian dissident, concerning allegations that a senior European politician was a former KGB *"asset"*. Together with Gerard Batten, a Member of the European Parliament, we were introduced by Bukovsky to Oleg Gordievsky, formerly deputy Head of KGB in London. A great deal of information came our way during the course of the meeting, but for quite some time we seemed to be skirting around the real reason for our being there. Eventually we got there, and the name I had previously been given finally came into the conversation. Our motives were questioned briefly before our two Russian friends made a call on a mobile phone. After some discussion, the phone was handed to Batten, with the words *"This young man will give you Romano Prodi... His name is Alexander Litvinenko"*.

The following month Batten denounced the former President of the European Commission - and at that time candidate for the office of Prime Minister of Italy - to the European Parliament in Strasbourg. Amongst the most serious of claims was that Prodi had in some way colluded in the protection of KGB agents allegedly involved in the attempted assassination of Pope John Paul II in 1981. This claim was supported by the Italian Parliamentary Commission, headed by Paolo Guzzanti, who concluded that the KGB and GRU (Soviet military intelligence) were involved in the assassination attempt. The Pope's personal secretary,

Cardinal Stanislaw Dziwisz also alleged in his book *A Life with Karol*, that the pope was convinced privately that the Soviets were behind the assassination attempt, writing that, *"all roads lead back to the Soviet KGB"*.

Calling for an enquiry into Prodi's alleged links, Batten stated that, *"Former senior members of the KGB are willing to testify in such an investigation, under the right conditions... It is not acceptable that this situation is unresolved, given the importance of Russia's relations with the European Union."*

No enquiry was ever held.

In November 2006, Alexander Litvinenko was admitted to hospital with suspected poisoning. Twelve days later he was dead, having been poisoned with Polonium. The man wanted by police in connection with killing is a former KGB officer who now sits as a member of the Russian Parliament.

The relationship between Russia's security forces and its government has changed since the fall of communism, and understanding the dynamics between the two is a crucial factor in deciding how we conduct our relations with that country. Russia is not a democracy as we in the West would define it, and attitudes within government and industry alike towards laws and contractual obligations differ fundamentally from ours. It is, however, a great and proud nation whose people have suffered dreadfully during its recent turbulent history. The position of power it occupied within the Soviet Union is gone, and its neighbours are looking westwards, restructuring their societies and economies, and joining the EU and NATO. This is extremely humiliating for Russia, which seemingly does not understand the

Western goal of peaceful interdependence based on the rule of law any more than many Western politicians understand the Russian mindset, which they perceive to be a threat to their security. Russia, I would argue, is highly unlikely ever to adopt the structures of a liberal democracy, and so we have no choice but to accept the presence on the EU's Eastern borders of a controlled state, currently being run by the same people who own it, and with little regard for international law or public opinion.

Some may describe 21st century Russia as "fascist". While it certainly satisfies many of the criteria classically associated with fascism, I nonetheless feel this to be a pessimistic evaluation, and in any case I abhor the use of analogies with the past in order to denigrate that which we may not fully comprehend now. I would point to the extreme economic conditions that followed the break-up of the Soviet Union - a situation that the Western nations both desired and contributed to, as being the catalyst for dramatic swings that saw, initially, forms of democratisation and liberalisation introduced at breakneck speed, followed by a swift reassertion of state control that appears to have swept aside many of the gains made.

The latter developments, of course, occurred under the jurisdiction of one man: Vladimir Putin. Following the resignation of Boris Yeltsin in December 1999, Putin became acting President of the Russian Federation. Calling an election in March 2000 - his rivals had been preparing for elections in June - Putin was victorious and was formally inaugurated in May. He was re-elected in March 2004, but only being allowed to serve two terms he was obliged to stand down in 2008. He oversaw a major restructuring of several aspects of the Russian political system, replaced the elected Governors and Presidents of the regions and republics with officials proposed by his own office, and by the end of his second term there remained little in the way of independent political power. Changes to the legal system have seen trial by jury abolished in some cases. The political and financial institutions have been seeded with Putin's former KGB associates, the independent media has been silenced, and journalists intimidated and murdered. On leaving the Presidential office, Putin became Prime Minister, and in many policy areas has been perceived as significantly more powerful than his successor as president, Dmitry Medvedev. Whilst his Machiavellian behaviour would not have been out of place in Western Europe in the early half of the last century, we need to understand that Russia is at a different stage in its development to its European neighbours. The evolution of the Russian polity differs from our own experience and history, driven by different priorities and values. Within the context of the Russian political system, and from the perspective of the Russian people, Putin has been a great success. He arrived on the stage at a time when there was no other world leader of any great note in Europe, or indeed anywhere else, and at a moment in history when European sovereign states are realigning themselves along federal lines. He has been quite clearly the strongest and most decisive political leader of the early 21st century.

I would argue that the most negative aspect of Putin's political legacy from both the Russian and foreign perspective is his suppression of potential rivals, both individual and corporate. The *competitive elitist* nature of politics should see new blood and new ideas rising to the surface ready to take the helm in the future. This is unlikely to happen under the present regime, and without that competitive struggle during which the strongest and most able develop their political skills, the next generation of leaders may not emerge with sufficient experience. This is likely to be to Russia's great detriment, as the result is likely to be further assumption of power by the state bureaucracy, and a dogmatic attachment to the past. Regimes and ideas that outlive their natural life spans seldom, if ever, serve their people well.

Gary Cartwright
Brussels
September 2009

Vladimir Vladimirovich Putin, Second President
of the Russian Federation, 2000-2008.
Photo courtesy of: www.kremlin.ru

chapter 1
resource wars

On the very day he took over presidency of the G8 group of nations, January 1st 2006, Russia's President Vladimir Vladimirovich Putin may have fired the first shots in a war. A very different war to those we have become familiar with, but one that we have every reason to fear: a resource war. Actually, this is nothing new; one of the earliest documented conflicts took place approximately 4500 years ago, when two Sumerian city states, Lagash and Umma, fought over the drawing off of water from the river Tigris for irrigation purposes. The word *rival* comes from the Latin *rivalis,* which means 'someone sharing a river'.

With the global demise of political ideology, in favour of a Benthamite *"What matters is what works"* approach to governance, future conflicts are again likely to come as a result of competition for resources. And what more valuable resource is there, in both political and economic terms, than energy?

On New Year's Day 2006 Putin shut off the gas pipeline supplying the Ukraine, ostensibly as punishment for siphoning off gas destined for Western Europe, although many observers interpreted this action at the time as being primarily a flexing of Russian political muscle. If Putin was waiting to see what the response from the West would be, he would have a long wait: The West acted, as if it were totally powerless.

We can assume that Putin, the former KGB Colonel, would have been much heartened by this impotence for he accelerated what is proving to be the most ambitious and successful power grab in history. Exactly one year later, January 1st 2007, a deal between Russia and Belarus effectively signalled the end of cheap energy supplies for former Soviet states. The latter would pay with immediate effect $100 per thousand cubic metres for natural gas, against the traditional price of $47 (roughly the price then charged for Russian domestic users.) Russia had demanded slightly more, $105, but agreed a deal which includes the transfer of a 50% stake in the Belarusian gas-transit monopoly, Beltransgaz, to Gazprom, the Russian state-owned energy giant. Minsk had stubbornly held on to Beltransgaz for many years but in the face a shutdown of supplies, Lukashenko's government capitulated. Belarusian threats to disrupt the transit of Russian gas to the EU proved worthless, for by stockpiling gas in anticipation of a repeat of the 2006 shutdown, and by refusing to give diplomatic support to Lukashenko, European states actually undermined the one ace the Belarusian dictator held up his sleeve.

On the very same day that the Belarusians capitulated, Gazprom also sharply raised the prices paid by Azerbaijan, Georgia, and Moldova, which, in 2005, had imported 8 billion cubic metres of natural gas between them.

Putin's actions between 2006-7 were soon to be repeated, with even stronger repercussions for those on the receiving end. In December 2008, Putin stated that *"the era of cheap energy resources, of cheap gas, is of course coming to an end"*, and on January 1st 2009, supplies to the Ukraine were again shut off. By this time, the EU was dependent on Russia for 25% of its gas requirements, and as temperatures plummeted to -10C, heating systems were shut off across the continent. Romania, the Czech Republic, Slovakia, Bosnia-Herzegovina, Bulgaria, Croatia, Greece, Hungary, Macedonia, Serbia, and Austria all reported a total halt of Russian-supplied gas, while Italy said it had received just 10% of its expected supplies. Slovakia, 100% dependent on Russia for its gas, was forced to declare a state of national emergency as a result of the crisis.

Russia blamed Ukraine, claiming initially that the dispute centred on unpaid bills, and then accusing the Ukrainians of siphoning off gas intended for the EU (80% of the EU's gas transits through Ukraine) and shutting down pipelines. Kiev claimed that the bills had been paid, that the pipeline taps were located on Russian soil, and that they were powerless to control the flow. Undeniably, however, the Ukraine had been benefiting from lower prices than the EU, paying $170 per thousand cubic metres. Russia sought to increase this to $250, still a good deal by comparison, as the EU was paying $400 at the same time. The Ukrainians however, were unwilling to accept the new price. According to political commentator Masha Lipman of the Carnegie endowment for Peace, this dispute was never about economics: *"Moscow cannot pretend this purely a commercial dispute"* she stated. *"There's little doubt that Russia is using its energy resources as a political tool".* Like other commentators, she pointed to the Ukraine's ambitions to join NATO and the EU as the catalyst for the dispute.

The empty chair conference...

Gazprom boss Aleksey Miller and Oleh Dubyna, head of Naftogaz, were said to be "talking", after an unexplained problem involving a diverted flight kept the Russian delegation away from a meeting in January 2009 in Brussels with Members of the European Parliament (MEPs).

Ukrainian deputy Prime Minister, Hryhoriy Nemyrya, attempted to explain to the anxious MEPs how the two states had managed to find themselves in such an impasse. He explained how an agreement on protocols for negotiation had been reached, based on two "pillars". The first was the nature of negotiation, which must be between governments only, excluding intermediaries, which he stated gave too much opportunity for corrupt elements to manipulate the process. The second pillar was an agreement on a gradual adjustment of the price paid by the Ukraine to reflect current market prices. However, unable to disguise his frustration, he declared that *"It is extremely difficult to conduct negotiations when you are faced with a moving target"*. The Ukraine had, in the course of recent negotiations, been presented with no less than four different price proposals. Russia also displayed a reluctance to see the transit price it pays the Ukraine – through whose territory 80% of Russian gas exports transit - to reflect the market.

British conservative MEP Charles Tannock asked how the Russians could justify raising prices at all given the plummeting prices of both natural gas and oil. *"Gazprom seems to be a branch of the Russian foreign ministry"*, he said, echoing other comments about the political nature of the dispute, before speculating on the need for Bulgaria to consider re-commissioning a mothballed nuclear facility.

"We cannot have our Bulgarian neighbours suffering like this", he asserted. Mr Tannock may have been unaware of the Belene nuclear power plant, in northern Bulgaria, construction of which began in September 2008. This nuclear plant is being built with € 3.8 billion of Russian money; one Russian company is a partner in the project, and a second Russian company is seeking to buy out 50% of the stake of the German partners in the project. This will be discussed further in a later chapter.

Ukrainian Prime Minister Yulia Tymoshenko attempted to address Russian allegations concerning the shutting off of supplies by her country by inviting EU Commission President Barroso to send monitors to inspect pipelines and metering equipment. The empty chair policy, if indeed that is what actually happened, was seen as a public relations mistake by the Russians. The Ukrainian delegation very clearly won the sympathy and support of EU parliamentarians who shared many of their frustrations and concerns. The question had to be asked: *to what degree does the Kremlin control Western Europe's energy supplies?*

"We will hang the capitalist with the rope he sells us."
– V. I. Lenin.

On July 18th 2006 'Federal Bill No. 117-F3 *"On Gas Exports"'* came into effect effectively institutionalising Gazprom's monopoly on the Russian gas industry and squeezing out foreign interests. The bill sailed through the Duma with little or no opposition; Putin's signature being little more than a formality. Very significantly, the legislation was technically initiated by politicians of all the main parties, including the fascist Zhirinovsky. The involvement of what are normally considered to be oppositional forces suggests that Putin was exercising an extraordinary degree of control over the Russian Parliament. Ronald Nash, chief strategist at investment bankers Renaissance Capital, stated that, *"Europe really does have to listen to what Russia wants, and obviously this law is a fine example of what Russia wants!"*

Gazprom's relationship with the state is beyond question: *"We intend to retain state control over the gas transportation system and over Gazprom",* Putin had told German Chancellor Schroeder in 2003. That same year he stated in 'Novaya Gazeta' *"The European Commission had better forget about its illusions. As far as gas is concerned they will have to deal with the Russian state".* Coupled with an almost fascistic zeal to exclude foreign influence from the Motherland, the *Rodina* in Russian parlance, Russia has been frantically buying up assets overseas. Russia presently owns up to 50% of shares in gas companies in Poland, France, Hungary, Slovakia, Greece, and Bulgaria. On August 29 2005, meeting with Silvio Berlesconi, Putin sought to clear the way for Gazprom to invest more heavily in Italy's energy sector. Gazprom is also known to have made attempts to take over Centrica, which owns British Gas.

In November 2006 Gazprom announced its intention to acquire not only electricity companies, but also grid networks themselves. Nikolai Ilyakhin, Director-General of Gazprom subsidiary *Gazpromenergo,* is reported by Deutsche-Presse-Agentur as saying that his company is engaged in talks with utilities in Greece, Moldova, and Bulgaria. Ilyakhin claims that Gazprom's control over Europe's generation and grid network assets will guarantee supplies of fuel from Gazprom.

In September 2006, Putin flew to Athens where he pressured Bulgarian and Greek leaders to *"proceed more quickly"* in joint plans to link the Black Sea and Northern Aegean with a new gas pipeline. He also wants to secure Russian involvement in a proposed Turkish-Greek-Italian gas pipeline, prompting the then US Secretary of state Condoleezza Rice to voice strong concerns about Russian involvement in European energy policy. Former US Vice-President Dick Cheney has also issued similar warnings.

Putin himself always proceeds very quickly indeed. Little more than two months after approving the laying of a new pipeline from Siberia to the Pacific, more than 250 kilometres had been laid. It is nigh on impossible to imagine the EU, or indeed any democratic polity, moving in such a decisive manner.

Flying directly from Athens to Capetown, Putin met with Thabo Mbeki, and days later Russian investment firm 'Renova' signed a *"whole range of documents"* which include an agreement to guarantee power supplies to United Manganese, in which Renova now has a 49% holding. (Manganese is used in steelmaking, and South Africa has 80% of the world's reserves.) A 'memorandum of understanding' was also signed between De Beers and Russian diamond firm 'Alrosa', two firms which between them account for 75% of the world's diamond mining. President Putin certainly tied up a lot of loose ends during his visit to Capetown.

In mid-2009, the Romanian power company *Romgaz* announced that Gazprom was to be its partner in the building of several gas storage facilities and thermal power plants.

Gazprom commences drilling in Kirinskoye field offshore Sakhalin.
Photo courtesy of www.gazprom.com

Economy minister Adriean Videanu stated that it was his country's intention to develop a joint energy strategy with Russia.

Sakhalin-2

The European Bank for Reconstruction and Development (EBRD) was one of a number of institutions that funded Sakhalin 2, a major offshore oil and gas project to the east of Sakhalin Island. The project has been one of the largest recipients of foreign direct investment in Russia's history. Led by Royal Dutch Shell, with the involvement of Mitsui and Mitsubishi Corp, the project has raised serious environmental concerns, with pollution having already affected fish stocks to the point where Sakhalin Islanders dependent on the fishing industry have been put out of work. In some fishing grounds, the catch has fallen by up to 70%. There are also concerns about loss of bio-diversity; the project is threatening the breeding waters of the critically endangered Western Gray whale, and Salmon spawning areas have already been destroyed.

The Russian attitude to environmental concerns, however, seems to owe much to the old communist mindset, which decreed that natural resources exist purely for man's exploitation, and that nature is there to be overcome, not particularly to be valued in any way. However, suddenly the world was presented with a *volte face*. Russia's 'Federal Service for the Supervision of Natural Resources' announced that it would seek to pull the plug on the whole project due to environmental concerns. Coincidentally, this threat came at exactly the moment that Gazprom was applying pressure to acquire a 25% stake in the project in return for giving

Shell access to the Zapolyarnoye-Neocomian gas field in Siberia. Gazprom had initially been offered a smaller stake, but with massive cost overruns threatening to impinge on profitability of Sakhalin-2, there was naturally a demand for a bigger slice of the cake. Eventually Gazprom walked away with 50% plus one share, leaving Shell with just 27.5%, and Japanese companies Mitsui and Mitsubishi with 12.5% and 10% respectively.

The facility was officially opened by president Medvedev in February 2009, although the first cargo of oil was exported from the Oil Export Terminal at Prigorodnoye in December 2008. When full production is achieved, Sakhalin-2 will have the capacity to meet a highly significant 5% of global demand for liquefied natural gas, although the figure of 8% was quoted speculatively when investment was being sought. Even more significantly, it might be argued, he who controls Sakhalin-2 will exert tremendous leverage over energy supply to Japan, Korea, and China.

There is much controversy at present over environmental issues surrounding the proposed German-Russian NEGP pipeline project. The Kremlin seems decidedly unconcerned about these particular issues at this stage, however.

chapter 2
democracy in peril

Alongside Bill No. 117-F3, which excluded foreign interests from crucial areas of the Russian economy, other legislation, which would have surely provoked harsh action had it been carried through by a less powerful state, has found its way onto the books in a rather unusual, and highly provocative, fashion.

The Russian political elite had been badly shaken by the "colour revolutions" that had taken place in Georgia and Ukraine in 2003 and 2004 respectively, and laid a significant amount of the blame for these events at the doors of foreign-funded Non-Governmental Organisations (NGOs). To avoid a repeat on Russian soil, in late 2005 the decision was taken to disable the NGOs by imposing strict registration and staffing criteria on them.

The bill, as would be the case with 117-F3 some months later, enjoyed overwhelming support in the Duma. The final stage, however, which involved the President 'signing off' the bill, took place in rather unconventional circumstances. On January 10th 2006 Putin signed the bill away from the glare of publicity, announcing the fact to the public only after a delay of some days. On the very day Putin signed the bill German Chancellor Angela Merkel was conducting an official visit to Russia. Merkel had previously expressed *"severe criticism"* of the proposed legislation. Would it not have been more diplomatic for Putin to have waited a day or two before signing, given that he was obviously in no hurry to tell his people about the bill *or was this deliberate provocation on Putin's part?* Chancellor Merkel's office declined to comment. Given the level of funding provided by the EU through the EU-Russia Co-operation Programme to Russian NGOs and other political actors, the EU should have been a little more concerned about the effects of this bill.

NGOs are considered to be a vital component of civil society, itself very important in the development and integrity of a democratic polity. Some estimates suggested that as many as 600,000 registered NGOs emerged in post-Soviet Russia. The Yale Centre for the Study of Globalization speculated that there may also be a similar number of informal unregistered groups operating. The removal of Western aid and assistance from many of these groups raised question marks over their continued viability. Although exact figures are not available, up to 2000 foreign NGOs were believed to be operating in Russia at the time the new legislation was introduced, although Duma deputy Alexei Ostrovsky, a co-author of the new law, estimated at the time that up to a quarter of Russian NGOs were receiving funding from abroad. These included environmental groups, human rights monitors and consumer advocates. In order to register under the new law, these organizations were required to fill out roughly 100 pages of documents, listing highly detailed personal information about each founder and each member. If any founders of the organisation were to subsequently die, the organization would then be required to provide death certificates. As of June 29, 2006, forty foreign NGOs had applied for official registration under the new law and not a single one was successful. Human Rights Watch, Amnesty International, the Danish Refugee Council, and two branches of Doctors without Borders were amongst the organisations forced to shut down temporarily due to problems with the registration process.

Amnesty International stated that: *"The experience to date has been that the law is unduly burdensome, diverting resources from substantive programs, while using a regulatory framework that can be arbitrarily applied, has key provisions which lack a precise legal definition, and sanctions that are disproportionate."* An aid worker in Chechnya described the NGO Law, with its excessive and impossibly difficult documentation forms, as *"Kafka's wet dream."*

In fact, the Council of Europe had reviewed an early draft of the law, and declared many of the provisions to be problematic. The Russian Government then revised the law, incorporating several of the recommendations made by the Council. Many of the more restrictive provisions remained, however, and the Russian Government also added new amendments in the final version limiting the rights of foreign NGOs and NGO members that were not in the original draft evaluated by the Council of Europe. These amendments potentially violate international and national law. Article 11 of the European Charter of Human Rights on freedom of information and expression, for example, institutionalises *"the affirmative duty to protect the right to association"*. The NGO law clearly contravenes this act, to which Russia is a signatory.

President Putin, in justifying the legislation, said, *"Whether these organizations want it or not, they become an instrument in the hands of foreign states that use them to achieve their own political objectives. This situation is unacceptable. This law is designed to prevent interference in Russia's internal political life by foreign countries and create transparent conditions for the financing of nongovernmental organizations."*

Russia's FSB security service chief, Nikolai Patrushev, a former associate of Putin from his St Petersburg days, blamed foreign-funded NGOs for fomenting coups in the former Soviet states of Georgia, Ukraine and Kyrgyzstan, and human rights and other groups were presented as being the vanguard of Western capitalist colonization. A paranoid public, with little understanding of how a free and democratic society functions, appeared to accept this, although even within Russia there are still voices brave enough to express dissent over the bill. This law *"...is aimed at establishing sweeping control over all organization of civil society... It will harm Russia."* said Yuri Dzhibladze, President of the Centre for the Development of Democracy and Human Rights.

Return of the Terror?

A third piece of legislation that calls into question the intentions of Putin's Russia is Federal Law No 153-FZ *"Introducing changes to the legislative acts of Russian Federation in connection with the passage of Federal law "On ratification of Council of Europe Convention on prevention of terrorism" and of Federal law "On counter-acting terrorism""* Passed by the State Duma on 5 July 2006 and approved by Federation Council on 14 July of the same year, this extraordinary and highly disturbing law outlines the powers the Russian state gives to itself to combat 'extremism' and 'terrorism'.

This bill states that:

"For the purposes of this Federal law the following basic terms are to be used:

1) Extremist activities (extremism):

a) Activities of public or religious associations, or other organisations, or mass media editorial offices, or private individuals, to plan, organise, prepare or conduct actions directed at:

- Forcibly changing the basics of the constitutional order and violation of integrity of Russian Federation,

- undermining the security of Russian Federation,

[...]

-conduct of terrorist activities or public justification of terrorism,

[...]

- Humiliation of national dignity,

[...]

- public libel against a person occupying a state position in Russian Federation, or a state position of a subject of Russian Federation, while the said person performs his administrative duties or in connection with his conduct of those duties, combined with an accusation of the said person of conducting actions specified in this article, provided that the fact of the libel is established by court.

[...]

- production and (or) distribution of printed, audio-, audiovisual or other materials (works), intended for public use and containing at least one of the qualifications listed by this article.

[...]

c) Public appeals to conduct the above activities, or public appeals and statements encouraging conduct of such activities, offering grounds or justification of conduct of actions specified in this article.

[...]

2) To amend the Article 15 with the Part Four as follows:

"An author of printed, audio-, audiovisual or other materials (works) intended for public use and containing at least one of the qualifications listed by Article 1 of this Federal Law should be considered a person conducting extremist activities, and is responsible for it in the order established by the legislation of Russian Federation."

Having effectively categorised critics of Putin's regime as 'extremist', the bill then allows for them to be dealt with as follows:

"The special assignment units of the Federal Security Service bodies may be used, by a decision of the President of Russian Federation, against the terrorists and (or) their bases located beyond the territory of Russian federation, in order to destroy a threat to the security of Russian Federation."

As former Soviet dissident and political prisoner Vladimir Bukovsky and ex-KGB chief Oleg Gordievsky recently commented in *The Times*, Putin has instigated a new law *"... enabling him to use his secret services to eliminate 'extremists' anywhere abroad..."* and has amended an existing law on fighting "extremism" in order to broaden the definition of the word to include anybody making *"libellous statements"* about his regime.

The new legislation, approved by the Duma in July 2006, also makes provision for the banning of opposition parties. *"You want to shut our mouths with the law on extremism, so that any statement we make can be interpreted the way one likes... you want opponents who stand in your way to be taken out of elections, you want to receive votes that don't belong to you...*" Ivan Melinkov of the Communist Party told the Duma.

It did not take long before the "extremists" began to be not merely silenced, but eliminated.

On October 7th 2006, the prominent journalist Anna Politkovskaya was shot in the head outside her home in Moscow. An outspoken critic of the war in Chechnya, she warned that Russia under Putin was sliding back towards Soviet-style dictatorship. She had previously been subject to harassment, abuse and even kidnapping at the hands of the security forces. Informed speculation is that she was assassinated in order to silence her, just two days before she was due to publish a report on torture by Russian forces in Chechnya. Photographic evidence of torture was said to have *"disappeared"*. Politkovskaya's murder was believed to be the 13th killing of a journalist critical of the regime since Putin took power in 2000.

Former President Mikhail Gorbachev said of her killing; *"It is a savage crime against a professional and serious journalist and a courageous woman. It is a blow to the entire democratic, independent press. It is a grave crime against the country, against all of us."* President of the European Commission, Jose Manuel Barroso, vowed to take up the matter personally with Putin, stating that; *"We want those who have assassinated Mrs. Politkovskaya, a great fighter for freedom of expression, to be brought to justice."* Possibly the most damning indictment of all, however, came from Oleg Orlov, head of *Memorial,* an independent human rights campaigning group, who resigned his position as an adviser to the Kremlin. He stated that; *"I wrote that I do not see any sense in remaining in the council…With regret I must note that my understanding of what is good for and what damages the Russian state … is fundamentally different from that of the president."*

In November 2006, former KGB Lt. Col. Alexander Litvinenko, a British citizen and outspoken critic of the Putin regime, was killed by a massive dose of the radioactive isotope polonium-210. On his deathbed the former agent issued a statement blaming the Russian state for his assassination, saying: *"You may succeed in silencing me but that silence comes at a price. You have shown yourself to be as barbaric and ruthless as your most hostile critics have claimed. You have shown yourself to have no respect for life, liberty or any civilised value."*

Russian parliamentarian Nikolai Kovalev has sought to blame the murder of Alexander Litvinenko - an act the British MEP Gerard Batten has called *"an act of war"* - on Russian oligarch and dissident Boris Berezovsky. The man actually wanted for the murder, Andrei Lugovoi, a former officer with the KGB's 9th directorate, now sits as a member of the Duma, where he enjoys protection from prosecution as a member of Vladimir Zhirinovsky's neo-fascist Liberal Democratic Party. Talking about the killing to Spanish newspaper El Pais, Lugovoi said, in December 2008: *"If someone has caused the Russian state serious damage, they should be exterminated. Do I think someone could have killed Litvinenko in the interests of the Russian State? If you're talking about the interests of the Russian State, in the purest sense of the word, I myself would have given that order."*

The Russian State Duma.
Photo courtesy of: NVO

Georgian tycoon Badri Patarkatsishvili, a close personal and business associate of Lugovoi, stated that he hoped his friend was innocent, but remarked that there is: *"no such thing as a former KGB agent."* Patarkatsishvili was a former member of Komsomol, the communist party's youth movement, who fled Russia to escape charges of fraud. He has been associated with Alisher Usmanov, sensationally named in connection with a variety of criminal activities by British MEP Tom Wise in the European Parliament - charges which Usmanov denies. Patarkatsishvili has been implicated in a rich variety of criminal activites ranging from mundane fraud to attempting to facilitate the breakout from jail of Nicolai Glushkov; the former Aeroflot deputy Director General, himself accused of fraud (Lugovoi was also implicated in an attempt to spring Glushkov from a hospital). Patarkatsishvili was impeached in 2007, as President of the Georgian national Olympic committee. He died in the UK in 2008, of natural causes.

Fascist Vladimir Zhirinovsky's spokesman and former bodyguard Sergei Abeltsev said of Litvinenko's murder, *"The deserved punishment reached the traitor. I am sure his terrible death will be a warning to all the traitors that in Russia treason is not to be forgiven. I would recommend to citizen Berezovsky to avoid any food at the commemorative feast for Litvinenko."* Abeltsev has a record of politically motivated violence; He publicly proposed to kill Yevgeny Adamov, former Russian atomic energy minister, to prevent him from disclosing state secrets in Switzerland. Abeltsev is now also a member of the Russian Duma.

"I don't agree that the Cold War is back. It has never ended," Lugovoi himself told the Los Angeles Times in January 2008.

In December 2006 Ivan Safronov, a 51-year old journalist, and defence correspondent for the newspaper *Kommersant*, published a damning report on the failures of the Russian Bulava Intercontinental Ballistic Missile. He revealed the continual failures of the system during test launches. This is the system hailed by Vladimir Putin as the next genera-tion in nuclear weaponry. Safronov was also known to be investigating the possibility that Russia was planning to sell arms to Syria, through a third party in order to avoid allega-tions of dealing with rogue states. He was duly questioned by the FSB. Subsequently he told colleagues he had been warned that the FSB would press charges of revealing state secrets against him. There would be no charges, however, as on March 2nd 2007, Safronov fell to his death from the 5th floor of his apartment building. He lived on the 3rd floor, and his hat and items of food that he had just bought were scattered on the stairs between there and the 5th floor. He was alive when he was found on the pavement, but emer-gency services refused to respond to calls for help; an ambu-lance arrived on the scene only after he had died. A verdict of suicide was returned by the coroner.

Ilyas Shurpaev was a 32 year old journalist with Russia's state TV Channel 1. A native of Dagestan, he had worked in Chechnya. Journalists are expected to be critical of regimes that the Kremlin does not approve of, but because he had written about positive aspects of Dagestan, Shurpaev was considered suspect. At 3.49pm on March 20th 2008 he wrote somewhat enigmatically in his blog *"I survived! Now I am a dissident! I don't know whether to laugh or cry..."* He specu-lated about moving to Israel to avoid a politically motivated prosecution. Exactly what Shurpaev did to upset somebody so badly is not known, but just hours after writing his blog entry he was murdered in his home in Moscow's Veshniye Vody Street. He was stabbed and strangled by unknown assailants who then started a fire at the scene in order to try to destroy evidence. Moscow police suggested that the killing was related to his work.

This culture of intimidation and violent suppression of criticism is in danger of becoming institutionalised, if it has not already become so. At local level, critical journalists are no longer safe: In November 2008, Mikhail Beketov, editor-in-chief of the Khimki-based independent newspaper *Khimkinskaya Pravda* was beaten almost to death in his own yard. Beketov was critical of the Khimki administration's decision to deforest a large area of the region in order to construct a motorway connecting Moscow with St. Petersburg. He had been subjected to numerous threats, and received serious head injuries during the attack, leaving him in a coma.

In December 2008, two unidentified men attacked and beat Zhanna Akbasheva, a investigative journalist for the independent news agency *Regnum*, in the North Caucasus republic of Karachai-Cherkessiya. She has a record of covering issues of corruption, and is a champion of freedom of the press. Following a story about local government corruption, in 2008 she was denied access to government buildings, and had her press accreditation removed. She was severely beaten and kicked repeatedly in the abdomen.

During the same month, Shafig Amrakhov, editor of the Murmansk-based online regional news agency *RIA 51* was shot several times in the head outside his home. He died in hospital on January 5th 2009. In February 2008, Amrakhov had publicly protested against the authorities' decision to deny him accreditation for the then President Vladimir Putin's last press conference as head of state. In his public letter widely produced in the local press, Amrakhov also criticized the economic policies of Murmansk Governor Yuri Yevdokimov.

On January 19th 2009, 34 year old Stanislav Markelov, described as a "prominent lawyer", was shot dead in broad daylight in a Moscow street. Markelov acted for the family of 18-year-old Chechen girl Elza Kungayeva, who was raped and murdered by Russian army Colonel Yuri Budanov in 2000. The officer obtained an early release from prison, and the young lawyer had appealed against this. The father of the murdered girl, now living in exile in Norway, said that Markelov planned to appeal to the Strasbourg-based European Court of Human Rights if Russia's Supreme Court turned down his new complaint against Budanov's early release. Anastasia Baburova, 25, a trainee reporter from Anna Politkovskaya's *Novaya Gazeta* who was investigating neo-Nazi activities in Russia, was shot along with Markelov. She died later of her wounds in hospital, the fourth journalist from the newspaper to be murdered since 2004. Defence analyst Dr. Pavel E. Felgenhauer stated that: *"In the opinion of the Novaya Gazeta staff, of which I am a member, the Russian security services or rogue elements within these services are the prime suspects in the murders of Baburova and Markelov. The boldness of the attack by a single gunman in broad daylight in the center of Moscow required professional preliminary planning and surveillance that would necessitate the security services, which closely control that particular neighborhood, turning a blind eye. The use of a gun with a silencer does not fit with the usual pattern of murders by nationalist neo-Nazi youth groups in Russia, which use homemade explosives, knifes, and group assaults to beat up and stab opponents to death. The offices of Russia's rulers President Dmitry Medvedev and Prime Minister Vladimir Putin have not issued any statements expressing indignation or offering any condolences after the two murders. This follows the usual behavioral pattern of the authoritarian Putin regime when its critics are murdered in cold blood."*

In February 2009, it was reported that Sergei Kurt-Adzhiyev, the editor of the now-defunct Samara regional edition of the independent newspaper *Novaya Gazeta*, reported police harassment of his two daughters. Indeed, this particular newspaper seems to attract a disproportionate degree of attention from the pro-Kremlin factions. For example, in April 2009 a package containing severed donkey's ears arrived at its Moscow offices with the message, *"From the administration of the president of the Russian Federation."*

In the city of Makhachkala, in the southern Russian republic of Dagestan, in June 2009, Nadira Isayeva, editor of the newspaper *Chernovik,* and four reporters were charged with *"extremism"*. *Rossvyazkomnadzor,* the state run media regulator, demanded that the newspaper be closed down. In the previous year, Isayeva had been charged following her use in an article of a quote from a guerilla leader, accusing pro-Kremlin regional politicians in Dagestan and Chechnya of corrupt practices. This was, under Federal Law No 153-FZ, potentially an extremist act against the state. The highly respected Moscow based human rights NGO *SOVA,* which is closely linked to the OSCE, issued a statement declaring that it had investigated the matter independently and could find no evidence of extremism in the article in question. SOVA subsequently found itself being accused of extremism, and Isayeva was subsequently charged with incitement to hatred against police officers.

Astonishingly, Valery Gribakin, a spokesman for the Russian Interior Ministry, told the independent news agency Itar-Tass that most journalists' deaths in Russia are not work-related, but rather the result of private disputes.

The name of Gribakin is not new to those who follow carefully the behaviour of the Russian state towards dissenters. Of particular concern is the way in which environmental protestors have been treated. It was Gribakin, then described as a "police spokesman", who dismissed as mere *"hooliganism"* an attack by neo-Nazis on an environmentalist protest camp which left one dead and others wounded in July 2007. The campers, near the city of Angarsk in the Irkutsk region in south-eastern Siberia, some 2600 miles east of Moscow, were protesting about the reprocessing of nuclear waste at a state-owned facility in the city. Uranium from a plant in Kazakhstan is to be enriched for export purposes at the centre, which is just 60 miles from the southern tip of Lake Baikal, the world's largest freshwater lake.

In Moscow two months previously, a demonstration by 2000 people opposed to the Putin regime was broken up by 9000 baton-wielding riot police. Dozens were subjected to violent assault, and dragged away to police cells. Gribakin described the incident as a *"provocation"*, and claimed that protesters had daubed themselves in tomato ketchup. Gribakin also described as a *"provocation"* an incident in November 2007 in Ingushetia, when three journalists and a human rights activist investigating the fatal shooting of a child by security forces two weeks earlier were abducted and severely beaten by masked gunmen.

Foreign writers engaging in Russian issues have also been subject to the heavy handed tactics of Russia's security services. Orlando Figes, writer and professor of history at Birkbeck, University of London, saw his book *The Whisperers* (Allen Lane) lose its Russian publishing deal in February 2009. The book dealt with the lives of ordinary Russians who had lived through the Stalinist period. In the Times (March 8, 2009) Figes wrote: *"I suspected there were political reasons, and my friends in Russia agreed. There has been a concerted campaign led by Putin himself to reclaim history and make Russians proud of their Soviet history - including Stalin."* In December 2008, armed men in masks raided Memorial, a human rights group that had helped Figes with his research, taking away materials, including testimonies from the Stalinist period. In May 2009 Medvedev established his 'Presidential Commission for Prevention of Falsification of History'. This body is dedicated to *"analyzing and suppressing all attempts at the falsification of history to the detriment of Russia."* It exists, effectively, to airbrush the crimes of the Soviet Union from history.

In March 2009, Boris Nemtsov, a former Deputy Prime Minister of Russia (1997 - 98), a candidate for the office of mayor of Sochi, was attacked in the street outside his campaign offices. Nemtsov is a former adviser to Ukrainian President Viktor Yushchenko, and had talked about recreating the Ukraine's *"orange revolution"* in Russia. He had expressed concerns about the way in which the Kremlin is organizing the 2014 winter Olympics in Sochi. As Mayor, he would have a great deal of influence over how resources are allocated, and this causes the regime some concerns, with some $12 billion having been allocated to the project. On 23rd March ammonia was thrown into his face by *"unknown assailants"*. Interestingly, police took more than an hour to arrive at the scene. Subsequently, as reported by the *Moscow Times* (6 April 2009), Sochi police seized some 125,000 election leaflets that were due to be distributed in the run up to the April 26th elections. Another candidate critical of the Putin regime, former ballerina Anastasia Volochkova, had her candidacy rejected because she forgot to put her date of birth on a bank deposit slip when submitting the required registration fee. Nemtsov had money paid into his account by an "anonymous donor", a technical infringement that could have seen him disqualified, and local TV stations were instructed not to carry coverage of his campaign, whilst lavishing attention on the official Kremlin backed candidate, Anatoly Pakhomov.

Nemtsov, who is a close ally of Garry Kasparov, another Putin critic to have suffered for his opposition, is reported to have said that he suspected the pro-Kremlin youth group, Nashi had been behind the attack on him.

It was hardly surprising that Anatoly Pakhomov, the Kremlins' favoured candidate, received 76.8% of the vote, against Nemtsov's 13.6%. Nemtsov and others have questioned the result. Exit polls conducted by his staff suggested that 46% of voters had chosen Pakhomov and around 35% of respondents had voted for Nemtsov. Such a result would have triggered a run-off election between Nemtsov and Pakhomov.

Both Nemtsov and the Communist Party, which received 6.7% of the vote, pointed to serious violations in the procedure of absentee voting: In one abuse described by election monitors, so-called *early voting,* voters were allegedly forced to vote by absentee ballot at their workplaces, and compelled to vote for the pro-Kremlin Pakhomov under threat of losing their jobs. Each ballot was placed in an envelope with the worker's name so that bosses could keep track of how each employee voted. The number of votes cast in this way was unusually high - 11% - as much as 100 times greater than the national average for elections, with 90% of these votes going to Pakhamov.

Russian parliamentarian Aleksandr Moskalets, deputy chairman of the Constitutional Law Committee, speaking to the newspaper *Vedomosti,* stated that laws governing electoral procedures might well be amended to expand early voting before the next national Duma elections.

According to Olga Shorina, Nemtsov's press-secretary, election monitors were blocked from some polling stations, and were barred from taking photographs and videos. In one instance Keith Gessen, an American journalist with the *New Yorker* magazine, was detained by police at a polling place where ballot stuffing had allegedly taken place. Yevgeny Rasshchepkin, a local Communist party leader, cited cases of people arriving at polling stations to find that a ballot had already been cast in their name. Yuri Dzaganiya, the Communist candidate, told the *Guardian* (26 April 09) *"These aren't real elections. It's the appointment of a Kremlin candidate with a little bit of local voting,"*

Nashi - Putin's youth movement.

In March 2005, Vasily Yakemenko, a young Russian politician with a flair for organization, announced the formation of a new pro-Putin movement, *Youth Democratic Anti-Fascist Movement "Nashi"*, or *"Ours!"* In 2004, Russia was shaken by the Orange Revolution in the Ukraine. Aware of the democratizing influence of civil society, and the support given to the process by youth movements, the Kremlin seemed to want to ensure the loyalty of its own youth, and to deny the democratic opposition the ability to harness their energy and support. Approximately $250 million was spent on the Nashi project during its first year of existence, although Yakemenko denied that this was state money, claiming that the organisation was funded by businessmen keen to win the approval of the Kremlin. Yakemenko had previously led the pro-Putin *Walking together,* a forerunner of Nashi, which fell apart following financial disputes, and a scandal involving dissemination of pornographic video cassettes by one of its senior figures. This was particularly ironic, as *Walking Together* used the sobriquet *"pornographic"* against its enemies in much the same way that Nashi describes everybody it disagrees with as *"fascist"*. The senior patron of the movement was Vladislav Surkov, later to rise to prominence in the Medvedev administration. Nashi was very quickly deployed to harass voices of opposition.

During the latter part of 2006, Sir Anthony Brenton, the British ambassador to Moscow, was subject to a six month campaign of intimidation by Nashi following a speech in July of that year on the subject of democracy to opponents of President Putin. Sir Anthony described the campaign against him as *"psychological harassment bordering on violence"*, and complained that it also affected his wife and children. The fact that Nashi had acquired a copy of the Ambassador's diary, and was able to shadow his every move, suggested a possible FSB involvement in the operation. *"Nashi's links with the Kremlin are well enough known,"* said Sir Anthony. *"Their leader has met with President Putin many times and one of his advisers was known to have been involved in its creation... Even if one were to accept that they are not directly controlled by the Kremlin, this level of influence suggests that the Kremlin could stop them if it wanted to."* Although Russia is a signatory to the Vienna Protocols, which require host countries to ensure the safety of diplomats, the government initially insisted that Nashi's actions were *"not illegal"*. Even when they later agreed to act, Nashi's campaign continued. Sir Anthony's speech, which highlighted the erosion of civil liberties in Russia, was known to have infuriated Putin.

In April 2007, Russia had a dispute with Estonia over the removal of a Red Army memorial, and the graves of fourteen soldiers to a cemetery in Tallinn. Estonians found the memorial an uncomfortable reminder of the Russian occupation and the repressions their people suffered during the Soviet era. Russia was opposed to the move, and the leader of the Russian Senate, Sergei Mironov, called for a resolution to cut all ties with Estonia.

In Moscow, Nashi struck out at the Estonian embassy. During April and May 2007, the Estonian ambassador to Moscow and several staff were so intimidated by Nashi that they fled the country. In the Russian-inspired riots in Estonia itself, one young man, a Russian national, was killed, and scores injured. Approximately a quarter of Estonia's population is of ethnic Russian origin, and some 50,000 Russian soldiers are believed to be buried in Estonian soil. In March

2009, a Nashi member, Konstantin Goloskokov, told the *Financial Times* that the group was behind a "cyber attack" on Estonia that caused that country's IT infrastructure to crash. Although any official involvement was always denied, Sergei Markov, a parliamentarian and Mr Goloskokov's boss, volunteered the information that one of his assistants had planned and implemented the attack at a conference earlier the same month. The significance of the incident is that this attack was on a NATO member state on Russia's border. Estonia is particularly vulnerable to such an attack, as much of its government is "paperless", and services are run online. Foreign and defence ministries were targeted, as were banks and newspapers. NATO has subsequently established a cyber defence facility in Estonia, funded and staffed by Germany, Slovakia, Latvia, Lithuania, Italy and Spain.

Although Nashi is believed to be in decline and possibly to have outlived its original purpose, as recently as July 2008 the organisation held a summer camp on Lake Seliger between Moscow and St Petersburg. Some 5,000 young Russians were in attendance, and Igor Shuvalov, appointed to the office of First Deputy Prime Minister in May 2008, lectured activists on the subject of economics, clearly confirming official government sanction for both the group and for the event. Amongst the *"patriotic events"* were a number of weddings, with newlyweds encouraged to procreate in order to raise the birthrate *a la* Soviet and Nazi eras. The Nashi website even has as its address **www.nashi.su**, the ".su" referring to the Soviet Union, harking back to an era looked upon nostalgically by the group's members.

Total devotion to Putin was always a pre-requisite for Nashi members, who numbered 120,000 at its height, and who attended training camps which bore a chilling resemblance to the Hitler Youth movement. When Russia celebrated its Independence Day on June 12th 2007, Nashi was the only youth organisation allowed onto Red Square. In December 2007, the *Daily Telegraph* reported that Nashi was funding a number of its members to travel to Britain in order to study.

The rise in politically motivated violence from the far right has been a major cause for concern in Russia in recent years. *Russia Today* speculated (Sept 5, 2009) that Moscow has its own version of the *Black Panthers*, the militant black supremacy group active in the US in the 1960s. In that month a young Muscovite, awaiting trial for a knife attack on two students on the metro was shot dead an hour before his trial was set to begin.In the same month, a gang of skinheads on trial included a seventeen year old girl accused of murdering an immigrant. A sixteen year old neo-nazi was arrested as he attempted to place a bomb near a war memorial, and was linked with other bomb and arson attacks. Four months earlier, in May nationalist leader Aleksandr "Belov" Potkin was sentenced to one and a half year's imprisonment for inciting ethnic hatred and violence. In summer 2008, a pact was made to form a coalition of far-right groups. At the time, Potkin (who styles himself as "Belov" – the name derives from the Russian word for "white) stated that Russia must *"be nationalistic or it will cease to exist"*.

In the context of *Nashi,* the question is, to what degree has the Russian state exploited this nationalist sentiment, with its violent and anti-democratic undertones?

chapter 3
the new arms race

So we can see that in both the economic and political spheres Putin has moved at breathtaking speed to secure his borders, whilst adopting an expansionist programme overseas. It gets worse. On May 10th 2006, in his annual State of the Nation address, Putin declared: *"It is premature to speak of the end of the arms race... Moreover it is today going faster; it is in reality rising to a new technological level."*

He went on to announce the creation of a *"million strong professional army"* to replace the present conscript force, as well as the strengthening of Russian nuclear forces. In his own first State of the Nation address, in November 2008, Medvedev was slightly to contradict Putin, saying that *"Russia will not be drawn into an arms race"*. However, he then went on to confirm the deployment of Iskander ballistic missiles in Kaliningrad, the cancellation of plans to withdraw three missile regiments from service in central Russia, and the further development of the nation's electronic warfare capabilities.

The Russian build-up includes the commissioning of two new strategic missile submarines, designed as launch platforms for the new Bulava ICBM, a variant of the TOPOL-M. This carries a 550 kiloton warhead and is considered by Western analysts to be an ideal first-strike weapon. TOPOL-M might be considered as similar to the US 'Minuteman-3', and the existing land based variant can be fired either from silos, or from highly mobile self-propelled launchers with an impressive off-road capability which potentially gives them a high survivability rate. It also has a significantly short engine-burn time, reducing its heat profile and making it difficult to detect by satellite on launch, enhancing its credentials as a first-strike weapon. The *Washington Times* (Nov 21, 2005), reported on a test launch of TOPOL-M from the Kapustin Yar missile complex in Southern Russia on November 1st, which confirmed the short engine burn and the manoeuvrability of the warhead. Missile defence systems, which rely on calculating warhead trajectory, are unlikely to be able to intercept such a weapon. TOPOL-M's chief designer Yuri Solomonov has stated that the missile can carry up to six independently targeted warheads.

Under the terms of START-II, Russian strategic rocket forces are allowed up to 300 TOPOL-M missiles, and it is anticipated that they will strive to fill this allotted quota. The first land based missiles entered service in 1998, although the project did then begin to fall behind schedule as the old regime struggled economically, and to date it is estimated that approximately 50 missiles are in service with four regiments. Col-Gen Nikolai Solovtsov, commander of Russia' Strategic Missile Force, confirmed in August 2005 that these first missile regiments were scheduled to be fully 'worked up' and combat ready at some point during 2006. The Russian business newspaper 'Vedomosti' has reported that 69 additional missiles are due for delivery in 2015. Rather interestingly, referring to the fact that Mikhail Gorbachev suspended the deployment of rail based strategic missile systems in 1992, Solovtsov described this as being because of *"negative political changes in the country"*, an interesting insight into the minds of Putin's general staff.

According to recent START exchange data supplied by Russia on ballistic missiles still in service, in October 2005 the Russian strategic forces included 815 strategic

RED SQUARE, MOSCOW 2008. Military parade marking the sixty-third anniversary of Victory in the Great Patriotic War.

*Photo courtesy of: **www.kremlin.ru***

delivery platforms, which can carry up to 3479 nuclear warheads. Strategic rocket forces have 545 operational missile systems that include missiles that can carry 1955 warheads. These include 85 R-36MUTTH and R-36M2 (SS-18) missiles, 129 UR-100NUTTH (SS-19) missiles, 291 road-mobile Topol (SS-25) systems, and 40 silo-based Topol-M (SS-27) systems. These are in addition to sea-based missiles. Russia's defence budget in 2006 was 2.75% of GDP. By comparison, France spends 2.5% and the UK 2.32%. In response to Russia's growing budget deficit, brought on by falling oil and gas prices, the government announced measures in mid-2009 to reduce spending by 15%. Medvedev and Putin both emphasised that state defence procurement would not be affected by this reduction.

Arming his allies.

In an echo of Cold War strategy, Putin armed the enemies of his potential enemies. President Hugo Chavez of Venezuela has proudly declared a *"strategic alliance"* with Russia. Chavez, who has a rather eccentric *weltenschaung,* believes that the US wishes to disarm and possibly invade his country. To alleviate his fears, Rosoboronexport, Russia's state controlled arms export company has supplied more than £1.6 billion of weaponry, ranging from assault rifles to highly sophisticated systems such as Mi-17, Mi-26, and Mi-35 attack helicopters. Venezuela has also been supplied with the state of the art Sukhoi Su-30 air superiority fighter, which is more than capable of giving US F-15s and F-18s a run for their money. Venezuelan pilots are also known to have evaluated the outstanding Su-35, and the Venezuelan ambassador to Russia, Alexis Navarro Rojas, stated in May of this year that talks aimed at procuring that aircraft are *"set to begin"*. In 2006, in an attempt to alleviate the effects of a US ban on weapons sales, Russia agreed to build arms factories in Venezuela.

In June 2008, during a visit to Moscow, Chavez signed a deal for 10 Il-76 transport aircraft, 10 Mi-28 attack helicopters, and three kilo-class submarines. The latter is considered one of the best diesel-electric submarines in the world, and is nicknamed "The Black Hole" by the US military due its ability to operate in relative silence. The submarines are believed cost somewhere in the region of $1 billion, and in September 2008 the Kremlin announced a $1 billion loan to Venezuela in order to buy weapons, but it is believed this credit was used directly to offset the purchase of Tor-M1 air defence missile systems for airfield defence. In October 2008, it was reported that a deal was struck for the purchase of a number of BMP-3 armoured personnel carriers, and that negotiations were being conducted for the acquisition of up to 500 T-90 Main Battle Tanks, one of the most advanced tanks in the world.

Venezuela is, of course, Latin America's main producer of crude oil, with a current production rate of 3.3 million barrels a day and reserves are estimated at approximately 270 billion barrels of crude - the worlds largest. Venezuela supplies up to 15% of the US oil requirements, but oil minister Rafael Ramirez has told the BBC that the country wishes to become less dependent on its trading relationship with the US. Chavez is supplying subsidised oil to Argentina, Bolivia, Paraguay, Cuba, and Uruguay, in an attempt to establish a Latin American bloc. Independent analyst and historian Alberto Garrido told the BBC that Chavez is also seeking to expand trade with China, also declared by Chavez to be a strategic partner. *"We've been producing and exporting petroleum for more than 100 years, but they were 100 years of domination by the United States. Now we're free and at the disposal of the great Chinese nation,"* he said in Beijing in 2004.

"Oil is being used to create or even buy a Venezuelan sphere of influence in Latin America and the Caribbean", states Jose Toro-Hardy, formerly a director of PdVSA, the state oil company. *"Chavez hands out oil and cash like there's no tomorrow, but in return he expects loyalty and solidarity..."*

Since coming to power in 1998 Chavez has survived a coup, a general strike, and a referendum on his leadership. In December 2006 he was re-elected for a third term, polling over 60%. His mandate is for six years, but it is widely anticipated that he will seek constitutional reform to remove limits on how many times he can be elected. He has stated that he intends to remain in power until 2021, by which time he plans to transform Venezuela from a capitalist to a socialist state. In an address to the fifth ministerial meeting of the WTO, Sept 12th 2003, Venezuelan Minister of Production and Commerce, Ramón Rosales, questioned the ability of the market to guarantee growth, or to tackle social issues including poverty. He stated: *"...It is necessary to reintroduce the idea of an appropriate level of state intervention, and to emphasize the role of public policy as tool without which it is impossible to achieve the stated goal of equitable, democratic, and environmentally sustainable development."* Whilst much of the agenda outlined by Rosales suggested a move to a more pluralistic society, his speech ended with the following words: *"The Venezuelan delegation will firmly and categorically insist that international agreements cannot limit the authority and the sovereign right of states to regulate, through laws and rules, the distinct service sectors that they consider to be of strategic importance in satisfying the basic and essential necessities of their populations."*

During a two-day visit to Moscow in September 2009, Chavez and Medvedev signed a number of deals relating to energy, foreign policy, and arms. The Venezuelan leader also announced, during a visit to the Russian leader's private residence, that his country would formally recognise the independence of the Georgian breakaway republics of South Ossetia and Abkhazia,

Speaking on the sidelines of a military exhibition in Argentina, SINPRODE-2006, in late September 2006, Sergei Ladygin, Head of Rosoboronexport's Latin American department, expressed his hopes that Russia's Sukhoi planes will also soon appear in other Latin American countries, referring to planned deals with Mexico, Brazil, and Chile, as well as the Venezuelan contracts. ISN Security Watch reported that on 2 August 2006, Russian Ambassador Yuri Korchagin met with Argentine Defence Minister Nilda Garre to discuss arms sales.

The Moscow-based Centre for Analysis of Strategies and Technologies (CAST) reported in its *Moscow Defense Brief 2005* (published 2006) that Rosoboronexport has established a maintenance centre for Mil helicopters in Mexico, which acquired its first Russian-built helicopters in 1995. That country's equipment is, however, based on that of NATO, and Mexico also has a small arms industry of own, mainly manufacturing weapons and ammunition under licence.

Military expansion in the Middle East.

In the Middle East Russia is moving to extend her influence through the expansion of naval forces in the region. The Syrian port of Tartus, which has been home to maintenance facilities for the Russian navy for many years, was dredged in 2006, and the port at Latakia is currently being widened. It has been suggested that the port at Tartus is to be converted in order to provide a home port for the Black Sea Fleet when it withdraws from Sevastopol in 2017. This explanation seems suspect however, as a new home for the Black Sea fleet is already under construction at Novorossiysk. Sources in the Russian Defence Ministry have also revealed that the missile cruiser *Moskva* is to be deployed permanently in the Mediterranean.

Both ports do have a highly significant strategic value as they face the receiving end of the Baku - Tblisi - Ceylan (BTC) oil pipeline. The strategic gains from this development are obvious, and make a mockery of the European Union's reliance on BTC as an *"alternative"* source of oil, and a guarantee of security of supply.

Moscow also plans to deploy an air defence system in Syria, based around the S-300PMU-2 surface-to-air missile. To be operated by Russian servicemen, this system will be able to provide air defence for Damascus, suggesting that Russia is seeking to pursue a Middle East policy symmetrical to that of the US in the region. The strength of President Bashar al-Assad's desire to have a protective Russian presence, thus limiting military options potentially available to Israel, is illustrated by the fact that no monetary charge is levied by Syria either for the facilities at Tartus or for the supply of power and water to the base.

Iran

In August 2006 the US government imposed sanctions against Rosoboronexport and Sukhoi, the state-owned aircraft manufacturer, accusing the companies of violating the Iran Non-Proliferation Act of 2000, which forbids any cooperation with Iran concerning weapons of mass destruction. The sanctions forbid US state agencies from dealing with the two companies, and private firms are forbidden to export military equipment to Russia. The catalyst for this move would appear to a contract made in July 2006 for Rosoboronexport to modernize 30 Su-24 front bombers which can carry tactical nuclear weapons. This contract is to be executed by Sukhoi. In response, Rosoboronexport issued the following statement:

"The sanctions imposed against the Rosoboronexport State Corporation and Sukhoi Company on August 4, 2006 by the U.S. Department of State, cause us extreme concern and misunderstanding. The alleged infringements incriminated to our Corporation for violation of the American internal law on the "Iran Non-proliferation Act" of 2000, that is aimed at preventing the spread of weapons of mass destruction to Iran, have nothing to do with the Rosoboronexport arms exports activities. The Corporation, as is well known, does not deal with the aforesaid types of weapons and their components. As to the Sukhoi aircraft manufacturer, the Company had not sold equipment to Iran since the 1990s. It should be emphasized that in our co-operation with Iran (the state, which is not a subject to the rule of international sanctions), we strictly adhere to the intergovernmental agreements, and do limit our relations by supplying exclusively defensive weapons. Many foreign companies,

including those from NATO member states, have conducted similar supplies.

The sanctions could have a negative effect on Russia-US co-operation in preventing illegal supplies of counterfeit Russian-designed military hardware reaching Iraq and Afghanistan, and could also affect other prospective projects within the US-Russian commercial relations. Being the sole state intermediary for Russia's export deliveries of defence-related products, Rosoboronexport carries them out in strict compliance with the Russian legislation, decisions of the Government and Presidential Decrees. The Corporation also strictly adheres to the spirit and letter of the standards of international law. Thus, the imposing of the afore-mentioned sanctions shall be considered as an unfriendly act toward the Russian state and an attempt to destabilize Russia's military and technical co-operation with other nations."

The sanctions against Sukhoi were lifted in November 2006. Analysts suggested the move was in reality intended to provide political incentive to encourage Moscow to support a US proposed sanctions package punishing Iran for its controversial nuclear program. *"The unexpectedly quick conclusion of WTO talks and especially the lifting of sanctions against Sukhoi show that bargaining for Iran is under way,"* independent defense analyst Pavel Felgenhauer told the *Associated Press* on Nov 19, 2006.

Russia had signaled that a US refusal to lift the sanctions could affect Security Council negotiations on a UN sanctions resolution against Tehran. *"The US met Russia half way and eliminated these complications,"* Felgenhauer said. *"In response Russia could also meet the US halfway."*

Within the context of international concern over Iran's nuclear programme, it should be remembered that the Bushehr plant in Southern Iran in being built by Russia. Deliveries of fuel to the plant began in December 2007. Sergei Shmatko, Head of Atomstryexport, the Russian firm behind the project, expects that the reactor at Bushehr could then come on line six months after delivery of fuel. Whilst Iran insists that the reactor has only a civilian purpose, the country has been test firing ballistic missiles. Spent nuclear fuel from the site will be shipped to Russia, and so the international community will have little chance of verifying that it is all accounted for.

On December 11th 2006, Russia's Deputy Industry and Energy Minister, Ivan Materov, announced that Gazprom had been invited by the government of Iran to set up new joint ventures for oil and gas extraction in Iran and *"third countries"*. Ongoing problems with late payments from Tehran have caused friction between the two states, but Gazprom is now very active in Iran, much to the annoyance of the US. In 2008 the Russian company announced that it would be developing the giant South Pars gas field, and that Gazprom Neft, the company's oil division, would be participating in projects in Iranian oil fields.

Afghanistan

In January 2009, President Medvedev announced that Russia might supply military equipment to Afghanistan. Despite the significant Western military presence in Afghanistan, there had been complaints that the country's own armed forces were being neglected. The West had presented Russia with an open door. Also allowing for the shipment of NATO weapons to anti-Taliban forces across its borders, Moscow announced a $2.3 billion loans package for Kabul, confirming and reinforcing the offer of arms and military advisors. Russia sees post-Taliban Afghanistan as a future ally, and US failure there could provide the Kremlin with the opportunity it needs.

Other arms exports...

Russian News and Information Agency (RIA Novosti) reported on December 7th 2006 that Russia expected to earn some $6 billion in arms exports in that year. Much of this revenue will come from the People's Republic of China, which still buys some 95% of its new weaponry from Russia. At time of writing, negotiations are underway for the purchase of 50 Sukhoi SU-33 Flanker carrier-borne fighters, a contract worth somewhere in the region of $2.5 billion. According to Pentagon analysts, hardware supplied to China in recent years includes transport, tanker, and attack aircraft, as well as various missile systems, including cruise missiles, and eight Kilo class diesel-electric submarines and two destroyers.

Rosoboronexport has signed a $3 billion deal with India for 140 Su-30MKI fighters to be assembled in India under a Russian license by 2014.

During the cold war, the Soviet Union supplied arms to various African nations that were ideologically opposed to the West. Under the present regime, Russia is seeking to re-establish those relationships. Moscow wants to establish maintenance facilities on the African continent for Russian manufactured arms and other military equipment. *RIA Novosti* has reported *"strengthening co-operation with*

*traditional African importers of Russian weapons -
Algeria, Libya, Angola, Ethiopia and Uganda - as well as
progress in co-operation with Morocco, Botswana, Namibia,
Mozambique and Burkina Faso."*

On March 10th 2006, at the end of a two-day visit to
Algeria, Vladimir Putin signed long-terms deals valued at
£7.5 billion. The Russian President also agreed to write
off £4.74 billion of Algerian debt. The Centre for Analysis of Strategies and Technologies (CAST) speculates that
this deal may involve the supply of Russian oil and gas
equipment. CAST further speculates that the US may seek
to interfere with the supply of Russian arms to Algeria by
strengthening economic ties with that country. US imports of
Algerian oil amounted to £10.3 billion in 2005. Algeria has
estimated oil reserves in excess of 11 billion barrels, and has
set a production target of 2 million barrels per day by 2010,
a goal it is likely to achieve given current rates of production
growth. This estimate of reserves may by conservative, as
Algeria has not yet been fully explored. The country is also
the world's third largest exporter of natural gas, and a major
supplier to the EU - as long ago as 2000, Algeria was already
supplying 20% of Europe's gas. The major foreign actor in
the Algerian gas industry at present is BP, but signs are that
both US and Russian interests are intensifying their activities, and that Algeria is actively seeking foreign investment
in its energy infrastructure.

Both parties are vague about the content of a *'Memorandum of understanding'* signed by Gazprom and the Algerian state controlled gas firm Sonatrach in August 2006.
The *Financial Times* (May 23 2006), reported on a warning
by Putin's former economic advisor, Andrei Illarionov, of

"a new form of gas cartel ... being developed by Russia and Algeria." On June 29, *Le Monde* warned that Gazprom *"is forging energy co-operation with Algeria, which could in the long run threaten European room for manoeuvre."* Italy is dependent on both Russia and Algeria for its natural gas supplies, and the August memorandum prompted the Italian energy company Sorgenia, to *"call on the government to open negotiations on the importing of natural gas from countries other than Russia and Algeria."*

Gazprom, and Putin himself, have openly called for the creation of a gas cartel, similar to OPEC, and in October 2008 Russia, Iran and Qatar, who between them control 60% of the world's gas reserves announced the formation of a 'Troika'. *"We are united by the world's largest gas reserves, common strategic interests and, which is of great importance, high co-operation potential in tripartite projects,"* said Gazprom chief Alexey Miller. As the world looked on aghast at the "re-election" of Iranian President Mahmoud Ahmadinejad in 2009, and the subsequent violent crackdown on opposition and suppression of the media, many in the West might have asked exactly what sort of strategic interests Miller was referring to?

A new Sino-Russian axis?

Russia's relationship with China is particularly interesting, especially in the light of the looming environmental crisis on China's borders. Himalayan glaciers have been dubbed the 'Third Pole'; with the largest concentration of glaciers outside the polar caps, which provide the water source for one-sixth of humanity. Now that water source is under threat from climate change. As the temperature rises, these great reservoirs of ice disappear. Great rivers such as the Ganges and the Yangtze are under threat, and could become seasonal. Already excessive melt is causing lakes to swell, with the threat of large scale flooding as banks burst. Flooding is becoming an increasing phenomenon in the region. Ultimately, as the rivers dry up, hundreds of millions will need to relocate in search of water. The most likely scenario is a movement of Chinese and Indian populations northwards, towards eastern Russia, where there is an abundance of resources and a very sparse population. The population of eastern Russia is very small; a mere 14 million people occupy its vast territories. In comparison, some 300 million of China's 1.3 billion people live in areas where there are chronic shortages of drinking water. In fact, whilst China has 20% of the global population, it has only 7% of the water resources, and some 40% of what it does have is so polluted that it is unfit for drinking. Presently, demand is being met by pumping water from deep aquifers, but these are running out, and anecdotal evidence suggests that wells around Beijing now have to reach down some 1000 metres to tap into fresh water. H.P.S. Ahluwalia, of the Indian Mountaineering Federation, studies glacial retreat on behalf of the Indian government. He predicts that in three to four decades the great rivers will become seasonal, precipitating a crisis.

Russia can supply the solution to this crisis, with some 70% of its natural resources located in its sparsely populated eastern region. In fact, Russia's population is dwindling at an extraordinary rate; with a birth rate of just 1.2 children per couple, the population is effectively halving with each generation. China also has an unusual aspect to its demographics – its gender imbalance. As a result of the 'guang gun' one child per family policy, introduced in 1978, China finds itself with 119 males for every 100 females. This means tens of millions of surplus males of military age.

Russian doctrine, however, still holds that the world will return to a bipolar state, and so a new Sino-Russian axis looks more likely than armed conflict. Indeed, on April 28th 2009, Russian Defence Minister Anatoly Serdyukov and his Chinese counterpart Liang Guangli announced a new era of Sino-Russian military co-operation, in the context of a growing strategic partnership between the two nations.

A possible solution to the crisis could be the peaceful ceding of territory to China. Russia has adopted such a pragmatic approach to such a problem in the past: issues of supply and defence were among the reasons why, in 1867, the province of Russia-America, known today as Alaska, was sold to the US government. Following talks in Moscow between Medvedev and President of the People's Republic of China, Hu Jintao, in June 2009, the Kremlin issued a press statement saying that "*Another important point of discussion was the contacts between our border territories and inter-regional ties. Today, they represent a significant share of our total trade turnover. The policy document on co-operation between Russia's Far East and East Siberia and the northeast of China should operate as an effective instrument. Work in these regions will continue in order to create an even better framework for co-operation. In addition, we must continue to work together on other important issues of trans-border co-operation, such as environmental protection and other issues.*

"*Our humanitarian co-operation is becoming more substantial as well. Not long ago, national theme years were organised in China and Russia. Currently, China is holding the Year of the Russian Language, and we will soon organise the Year of the Chinese Language in our country. The Festival of Chinese Culture will be opening in the Bolshoi Theatre today, to honour the 60th anniversary of the establishment of diplomatic relations between our countries. In addition, we will be holding other events in the humanitarian sphere. This is a very good foundation for co-operation between our countries and our peoples, and we will continue on these issues as a priority... We are about to set up a co-operation programme between the northeast China and Russia's Far East and Eastern Siberia, in order to launch and implement trans-border and infrastructure projects in our border regions, to the benefit of both our nations.."* Ties between the two countries are becoming noticeably stronger.

The city of Vladivostok, hemmed in between the Chinese border and the Pacific Ocean, has seen its population fall to 594,701 in 2002, from 633,838 as recorded in the 1989 census, although this figure is rising again due to an influx of Chinese and Koreans. In the early part of the 20th century the majority of inhabitants were Chinese, but all foreigners were actually deported from the city in 1958, and until 1991 only Soviet citizens were allowed to live there. Populations are already on the move in the region, and in the near future Vladivostok could well revert to its original name: Hǎishēnwǎi.

chapter 4
georgia and beyond

A gangster state, its people gripped by patriotic fervour -
Russian tanks invade - diplomatic relations at all time
lows - sabotage behind the lines - UK defences being probed -
Naval blockades and US warships in the Black Sea -
nuclear missiles targeted at Poland - Europe cannot agree
on a response.... and it all happened in a single month,
August 2008.

Facing imminent economic collapse and seeing only
enemies beyond its own borders, the Kremlin needed to do
something to divert attention away from the nation's economic woes. When the Russian military poured into Georgia
on August 8th, parallels were inevitably drawn with the Cold
War, but how serious was the crisis? Was the West facing
war with Russia?

We were certainly far less close than during the 1962
Cuban missile crisis, but the signals being sent out were
frighteningly similar. New alliances were hastily formed,
and battle lines drawn. Russia had lost the support of Serbia, Ukraine, and of course Georgia, not to mention those
former client states that are now members of the EU and
NATO. This was not only humiliating for Russia, but also
posed a perceived security threat. It is almost on a par with
half of NATO defecting to the Warsaw Pact during the cold
war. Ukraine, perceived by Russia as being within its traditional sphere of influence is edging ever westwards, following its democratisation. When observing this phenomenon,
one needs to remember that when German troops entered

the Ukraine in 1941 they were welcomed as liberators, not enemies. Self-determination has long been the greatest desire of the Ukrainian people; Russia traditionally overestimates the closeness of its relationship with its neighbour.

Deputy Prime Minister of Ukraine Hryhoriy Nemyrya stated that Ukraine supports the sovereignty and territorial integrity of Georgia. His press-service quoted him as saying, *"Ukraine has supported and supports the sovereignty and territorial integrity of Georgia. This position remains fundamental and invariable"*.

Ukrainian President Viktor Yushchenko called Russia's decision to recognise Abkhazia and South Ossetia unacceptable. Yushchenko then said that Ukraine must increase its defensive capabilities and pursue its bid for membership of the NATO military alliance. In strong words that will have infuriated Moscow, he condemned the Russian invasion stating that, *"What has happened is a threat to everyone, not just for one country. Any nation could be next, any country. When we allow someone to ignore the fundamental right of territorial integrity, we put into doubt the existence of any country."* President Yushchenko expressed hopes that the international community will join forces in restoring the territorial integrity of Georgia, and has effectively thrown down a gauntlet to Moscow by claiming his country is prepared to take an active part in this process.

French foreign Minister Bernard Kouchner warned that after Georgia, other ex-Soviet republics like Ukraine – the Crimea in particular - or Moldova risk finding themselves in the Kremlin's sights. It is an *"extremely dangerous"* problem, he warned. Former US Assistant Secretary of State Richard Holbrooke said *"Putin's next target will be Ukraine"*, and fears have been expressed that a potential flashpoint could be the Russian naval base at Sebastopol. Former head of KGB Oleg Gordievsky stated that, *"An attack on the Crimean Peninsula is highly likely, because they realise their reputation is ruined and they go on the principle that they don't want to be liked - they want to be feared. NATO should be ready to respond with weapons to attacks on Ukraine. If they don't it will be like the year 1938"*. Russia, however, then diverted Western eyes away from Ukraine with a threat to target Poland with nuclear weapons in response to that country allowing the US to site anti-missile defences there.

Although the performance of the Russian military in the Georgia conflict was widely regarded as being considerably better than in recent past conflicts such as Afghanistan and Chechnya, it was apparent to all observers that Russia is still a long way from having an army on a par with those of the NATO countries, with Russian troops being described by one journalist as *"Mad Max meets Stalingrad"*. Russian generals do seem to be preparing to fight the last war, and the sight of tanks trundling along roads in single file would have thrilled any Apache or A-10 pilot. Logistics were poor, especially given the long build-up time afforded the troops by exercises in the area. Discipline was also an issue, with widespread reports of looting and physical violence against civilians.

This all prompted another announcement, in December 2008, of $142 billion to be earmarked for modernising the armed forces. It is unclear as to whether this announcement by deputy head of the military-industrial commission Vladislav Putilin referred to new spend, or if it was a re-announcement of existing commitments. With the Russian budget in serious deficit since the fall in the price of oil, the latter seems more likely, despite assurances from Medvedev and Putin that defence budgets will not be cut. Defence Minister, Anatoly Serdyukov, argued at the same time for a radical overhaul of the military, turning it into a smaller but more mobile and better trained and equipped force.

Four months after the conflict, in December 2008, Russia engineered the removal of European monitors from Georgia. The Organisation for Security and Co-operation in Europe (OSCE) was forced out of Georgia by Russia, which wanted the organisation to treat South Ossetia and Abkhazia as sovereign nations. Russia was the only one of the OSCE's 56 member states to recognise the disputed enclaves as separate nation states, but the organisation requires unanimity, and so Russia was able to block any extension of the presence in Georgia, where its remit had been to assist the government of Georgia in the fields of conflict settlement, democratization, human rights and the rule of law.

OSCE chairman, Alexander Stubb, had proposed a package whereby South Ossetia would have a separate OSCE office, running operations in parallel. If this was unacceptable, then a three-month extension of the present arrangement was suggested in order to give time for further negotiation. Both proposals were rejected by the Kremlin, and the operation came to an official end on December 31st. Then in June 2009,

Moscow vetoed the extension of the UN observer mission's mandate in South Ossetia. The ending of this 16-year long mission made it virtually impossible for the international community to monitor the activities of Russian troops in the region. Sergei Bagapsh, installed by Moscow as President of Abkhazia, stated that all EU and OSCE observers must leave the enclave, and that only Russian monitors would be allowed. Eight thousand Russian troops were to be deployed, presumably in this capacity.

Bagapsh has very strong pro-Kremlin credentials, having been head of a Soviet collective farm, director of information for the Central Committee of Komsomol, and Secretary General of the Communist Party of the Ochamchira region. His deputy, Raul Khadjimba, is a former KGB officer, with a hardline stance towards the West, and a history of embroilment in controversial election results.

A rather interesting press release issued by the government of Abkhazia in November 2008 announced the culture festival "Abkhazia - country friends". This would give Abkhazians the chance to show solidarity with Russians, who would get the chance to see televised coverage of Abkhazian culture, emphasising their mutual roots in the Orthodox Church. Such propaganda is reminiscent of the old Soviet Union, but remains popular fare in the provinces. What is particularly interesting is the statement that *"The implementation of this event, no doubt, will be a step in the fulfilment of orders, which were given in April 2008, by Russian President Vladimir V. Putin, the Ministry of Foreign Affairs of the Russian Federation, and the Russian government for co-operation in trade, economic, social, scientific and technical fields in the field of information, culture and education, including the involvement of Russian regions"*. The events are not only stage managed by, but also funded by the Russian Ministry of Foreign Affairs. They clearly indicate Russia's willingness to exert influence over the political life of another sovereign state, as legally Abkhazia is still Georgian territory, although the press release suggests that Putin considered it to be a *"Russian region"*.

On April 30th 2009, Russia signed a formal five-year agreement on mutual protection of borders with Bagapsh and President Eduard Kokoity of South Ossetia. Under the terms of the agreement, Russia will supply aid to train security personnel and border guards. After the signing of the agreement Russia's FSB, Abkhazia's State Security Service, and South Ossetia's Committee for State Security also signed agreements on co-operation. NATO spokesman James Appathurai, speaking in Brussels, condemned the agreement as being in clear contravention of the ceasefire agreement brokered by the EU following the short war, and stated that: *"These actions by Russia are not in the interest of long-term peace and stability for all the people of the South Caucus region"*. Less than two months later, General Nikolai Marakov, Chief of General Staff, stated that the originally planned deployments were unnecessary, and that Moscow would scale down its planned presence in the two breakaway provinces. Whilst this is the news that the international community wanted to hear, the expulsion of monitors and observers means that it cannot be taken at face value.

In September 2009 tensions were rising in the region. The Georgian army was accused of firing mortar shells at an observation post in South Ossetia, an allegation denied by Tblisi. At sea, the Georgian navy was intercepting and seizing ships bound for Abkhazia, which it continued to claim as its own territory, and which is dependent upon imported fuel. Abkhaz President Bagapsh took the step of ordering his forces to attack Georgian ships entering Abkhaz waters. Whilst Abkhazia's navy is small, with just a handful of patrol vessels, the Georgian navy is also weak, and Bagapsh has stated that Russian help would not be necessary, although the Russian coastguard had made a commitment to protect Abkhaz waters. Political backing from Moscow, however, was quickly forthcoming, with the Russian foreign minister condemning Georgia's actions as *"nothing other than outrageous violation of the Law of the Sea Convention of 1982 and acts of international lawlessness".*

Dozens of ships were seized, with the skipper of one Turkish vessel receiving a 24-year prison sentence for "smuggling". Turkey is Abkhazia's most important trading partner.

Moldova.

President Medvedev met with Moldovan President Vladimir Voronin, the world's only elected communist head of state, on August 21 2009. Discussions apparently centred on economic affairs, with the Russian President lamenting the deterioration in relations between the two nations in recent years.

Voronin, a 68 year old baker of Romanian descent, had been playing a dangerous game; he had upset the Russians by reneging on his support for their plans to federalise Transnistria in 2004, and subsequently ordered an economic blockade of the troubled region. He had also previously committed his country to increased integration with Europe, and co-operation with NATO. These are dangerous ambitions, as Georgian President Mikheil Saakashvili discovered to his cost in August 2008.

However, in return for Russian support, Voronin was prepared to abandon his principled stance on Transnistria, and along with Medvedev and the Russian-installed *"president"* of Transnistria, Igor Smirnov, he signed a Russian-drafted joint declaration, in March 2009. This was probably a very wise move, with elections in April of that year, which were far from a foregone conclusion, and Voronin's position looking somewhat uncertain. The declaration primarily concerned ongoing negotiations over Transnistria's position regarding its unrecognised declaration of independence, and ensured the continued presence of Russian troops in the region. Following an OSCE agreement in Istanbul in 1999, Russia was committed to withdrawing its troops, having fought there in the brief war of 1992. Voronin made it possible for Moscow to stonewall, and delay any withdrawal. Indeed, Russia could manipulate the situation, and present its own forces as representing the will of the OSCE. Following the agreement, Medvedev went on television to praise Voronin for making the deal possible, thus giving him a much-needed boost in the April elections. Although his communist party was out-polled by a pro-western alliance, Voronin remained well placed as acting President.

On the one hand, we might conclude that Voronin's deal ensured the survival of Moldova's democracy by avoiding the possibility of Russian intervention, and the installation of another Kremlin sponsored *"President"*. On the other hand, the EU must now accept that Russian troops are likely to remain on Moldovan soil for the foreseeable future. Europeans might ask how it is that Russia can choreograph events so skilfully whilst the EU remains blinkered and startled in the starting blocks. Moldova had expressed an interest in integrating with the EU, with which it shares borders, and yet Moscow managed to draw the small nation back into its fold so deftly. In the early 90s, after the overthrow of the communist regime, there was talk of Moldova and Romania reuniting, with 44% of Romanians in favour of such a move. Now the old Soviet era lines are being firmly re-established. The uncertainty over which way Moldova should look for its future claimed one political victim in September 2009 – Voronin himself. Stating that he had little confidence in the ability of his own administration, after several days of confusion, he resigned on September 11th.

This re-alignment was followed by an interesting development, which should be viewed not only in the context of the Moldovan position, but also in that of Medevedev's law on "historical revisionism". Many observers believe that this is little more than an attempt to whitewash the crimes of the Soviet Union, particularly those committed under Stalin. It would appear that Moldova's schools are also being encouraged to reassess the Soviet era, and that this has not been well received by that country's academics. The Association of Historians of Moldova has recommended that teachers should not use newly introduced school curriculum programmes, claiming that they are a deviation from the historical truth and represent *"a refection of the Communist ideologue"*. The Association highlighted the fact that the Ribbentrop-Molotov Pact, whereby the Stalinist government annexed Romanian territories, is excluded from the new curriculum. We must hope that they do not pay too high a price for their academic integrity.

Cold War revisited.

Russia is also militarily active along its Northern borders with NATO. In August 2007 Putin ordered strategic bombers to resume the long-range patrols that were a feature of the Cold War. Norwegian and British fighters are now regularly scrambled to intercept the ageing bombers, as they fly over the Norwegian and North Seas. As many as eleven aircraft have been involved at any one time, with a Tupolev TU-160 'Blackjack' bomber from Engels Air Base near Saratov on Russia's Volga delta penetrating to within 20 miles of the British coast unchallenged in late 2007.

Aircraft are also resuming patrols towards Guam in the Pacific, and in February 2009 a TU-160 was intercepted approaching Canadian airspace. Canadian Prime Minister Stephen Harper reacted angrily to the incursion, which occurred 24 hours before US President Barack Obama was due to visit Canada, saying *"I have expressed at various times the deep concern our government has with increasingly aggressive Russian actions around the globe and Russian intrusions into our airspace...This government has responded every time the Russians have done that. We will continue to respond; we will defend our airspace."*

The routes being flown are basically cold war bombing routes. Following the break up of the Soviet Union, the flights stopped, primarily due to lack of resources. The aircraft involved are mainly very old, although the TU-160, a supersonic bomber with a range of 7,640 miles without refuelling, entered service in 1987. There are, however, believed to be less than 20 serviceable airframes, although further deliveries are anticipated at the rate of two every three years.

In an interesting twist, in August 2009 Russia's top general, Nikolai Makarov, the chief of the General Staff, announced that the Russian navy wanted to buy a French helicopter carrier. In what would be a landmark deal, the navy planned to buy a Mistral-class helicopter carrier — capable of carrying 16 helicopters, 40 tanks or up to 900 troops — and then to jointly produce three or four additional carriers with France in Russian shipyards.

"Before the year's end, we plan to obtain contract agreements with a French company allowing the construction and purchase of this ship," Makarov told reporters in the Mongolian capital, Ulan Bator, where he was travelling with President Dmitry Medvedev. This would be the biggest ever foreign military purchase for Russia, which has traditionally relied on the Soviet-era principle of producing all its military equipment domestically, albeit often with the aid of plans and blueprints "acquired" from NATO countries. *"No country in the world can do everything on its own",* Marakov said. *"Something will have to be purchased from abroad."*

The French navy currently has two of the 21,300-ton carriers in service, with one more under construction at the time of writing, at the Chantiers de Saint-Nazaire dockyards. Speculation that Russia was interested in buying the helicopter carrier, first surfaced in Vedomosti and Kommersant earlier in 2009, but Russian officials initially denied the reports. Russian defence analysts were also known to have questioned the expediency of such a costly purchase in the name of national security. Any military conflicts likely to involve Russia would be with its neighbours, which would require land troops and equipment rather than a sea vessel, they argued.

Sponsoring terrorism abroad.

Russia also continues to undermine its rivals abroad by promoting terrorism. As well as violent acts against the state in Abkhazia and South Ossetia by separatists, which caused the Georgian response that precipitated the Russian invasion, Kurdish separatists with traditional links to Moscow attacked an oil pumping station just outside Georgia's borders, in Eastern Turkey, 72 hours before the invasion. Were they also acting on the Kremlin's orders? Oleg Gordievsky states that *"The FSB (formerly the KGB) is massively present in South Ossetia. The crisis there has been manipulated by them."* Gordievsky has also confirmed that leading PKK figures have been trained in Soviet military academies and schools, and that the Kremlin would not find it difficult to influence that group.

Putin has profited politically from "beneficial crises' in the past. In September 1999 the first of a series of apartment block bombings took place in Moscow. On September 22nd, an attempt at planting another bomb in an apartment block in Ryazan was thwarted. Two days later, the perpetrators were arrested. On being taken into custody they produced FSB ID cards. The war launched by Russia in Chechnya in response to these "terrorist" acts helped bring Putin to power. The head of the FSB until a few weeks before the atrocities was Vladimir Putin himself. He was replaced by Nikolai Kovalev, who is now a member of the Russian Duma, where he sits as a member of the United Russia Party, the Chairman of which is - Vladimir Putin.

On April 6th 2009, Associated Press reported that Sulim Yamadayev, a Chechen opponent of the Kremlin's puppet president Ramzan Kadyrov, had been gunned down in Dubai on March 28th. Lt General Dahi Khalfan Tamim, Dubai's chief of police, stated that Russia was "...*responsible for untying the knot of this crime*". Two suspects were arrested, but Tamim reported that four others had fled to Russia, one of whom, Adam Delimkhanov, is a member of the Duma, the Russian parliament. Delimkhanov's staff allegedly supplied the murder weapon, according to one of the suspects taken into custody. The *Times* claimed that "Members of parliament are rarely accused of murder but in Russia it is becoming a trend..." (April 7, 2009).

Yamadayev's brother, Ruslan, himself a former parliamentarian, was shot dead in September 2008 near to Putin's Moscow offices, after attending a meeting at the Kremlin. The car he was driving actually belonged to his brother, and initial press reports named Sulim as the victim of the shooting.

chapter 5
russia and the eu

Through its EU-Russia Co-operation Programme, the European Union is the largest single donor to the Russian Federation, having committed more than €2.7 billion between 1991 and 2006 for over 1500 projects. The Programme supports the Russian Federation primarily within three programme areas: national programmes, cross-border and regional programmes, and special initiatives to enhance nuclear safety. Initially funded through TACIS (the programme of technical assistance to CIS countries), since January 2007 it has received its funding through a new regulation for the European Neighbourhood and Partnership Instrument (ENPI). As part of this transition, a greater emphasis is placed on co-funding and on strategic projects as defined by the European Commission and Russian Ministry for Economic Development and Trade.

The indicative budget available from the European Commission for the seven EU/Russia partnership programmes covered by ENPI from 2007-2013 totals €307.448 million. Co-financing from Russia for the relevant projects during this period is "foreseen" to amount to €122 million. Russia has been the single biggest beneficiary of EU support to the countries in the post-Soviet region receiving about half of all funding. Large projects are approved after discussions with the Russian Government and the project partner, often a Governmental department or a regional administration. The Russian Government and the European Commission approve the terms of reference of these projects, and invitations for expression of interest are published. Respondents may be based in the EU, Russia, future EU-state or EU beneficiary country. EU-funded national programmes address issues that primarily or only affect Russia, particularly those issues regarding the development of free-market and democratic practices. All programmes are developed with the Russian government and seek to complement the government's own programmes.

The EU-Russia Co-operation Programme supports projects with a regional impact through its cross-border and regional programmes. Many issues broadly affect more than one country and these programmes seek to address these issues and coordinate responses between the EU and national governments. Into this latter category fall issues such as sustainable management of natural resources, trade and investment, and justice and home affairs.

Following the explosion at Chernobyl in 1986, concerns over nuclear safety have been at the top of the European agenda. In Russia alone, the EU-Russia Co-operation Programme spent €310 million on nuclear safety programmes from 1991–1998. Russia's civil nuclear industry is a major source of employment, accounting for approximately 300 000 people. The military sector is estimated to be twice as large, and the EU funds the transition of scientists from the military to the civil sphere, thus, one might argue, allowing the Russian government to concentrate its resources on the military sector.

Future EU-Russia relations

The EU is, or at least aspires to become, a post-modernist state. It evolved as an attempt to distance itself from traditional nationalism, and all the problems of the last century that stemmed from it. The post-modernist state does not emphasise sovereignty, it places no priority on balance of power and rejects the use of force as a means of resolving disputes. It actively seeks to evolve into a new form of polity, away from the traditional concept of the nation state and the Westphalian order.

Russia, on the other hand, identifies with a 19th century concept of statehood. Ivan Krastev, chair of the Centre for Liberal Strategies in Sofia, commented in *The American Interest* (Nov/Dec 2008) that *"For Moscow, postmodernism is what vegetarianism is to cannibals: an irritating irrelevance."* Russia sees the EU as a temporary phenomenon, destined to failure. The Russian policy of striking bilateral agreements with EU member states is not just one of divide and conquer; the Kremlin quite simply does not think the project will stay the course. Russian observers point at the Commission's inability to sell the Constitution/Lisbon Treaty to the people without breaking its own rules as just one sign of the weakness inherent in the entire project. The EU's behaviour following the Georgian crisis of 2008 will only have confirmed the Union's weakness and inability to act decisively: although the EU brokered the August ceasefire, Russia subsequently annexed two Georgian provinces, refused to withdraw their troops, and then engineered the removal of international monitors. What was the EU's response to these provocations? Precisely nil. Not so much as a sanction. It is unlikely that this display of total impotence would have been missed by Iran, either.

Yeltsin's post-communist government was never really democratic, nor was it intended to be. It merely feigned it in order to garner Western largesse. In fact, in retrospect, we can see that liberal democracy was never likely to emerge in the initial post-communist years. Russian civil society is weak, and there was little support among the populace for any alternative form of governance at all. None of the myriad of newly emerging political parties had any real support, and only the Communist Party itself, reconstituted in 1993, could claim any significant following with some 500,000 members. The final years of communism had also seen an economic slow down, with a fall in economic activity in 1990, with output falling by as much as 50% over five years - the biggest decline that any major nation has suffered outside of wartime. Whilst many former Soviet states recovered quickly from this, Russia did not. The presence of nominally democratic institutions was of little importance to the 36 million Russians living below subsistence level, according to government figures. Other worrying signs began to appear: life expectancy fell, serious diseases, once controlled, were starting to reappear. In 1992, for the first time since the Second World War, the Russian population began to fall. The presence of competitive elections, formally independent courts, and an independent media may have suggested at least a form of liberal democracy, but this was nominal at best. In reality parliament had very little control over the government, the political parties were very weak, and the independence of the courts was highly questionable. Government itself, especially at local and regional level, was run by former communist *nomenklatura* and organised criminal groupings.

The post-Yeltsin Russian state is built upon three pillars: natural resources, memories of the Second World War, and anti-Americanism. Vladimir Putin seems to claim continuity with both the Tsarist and Soviet past, hence his use of the Orthodox Church as a political tool. Patriarch Alexis II (1929–2008) maintained a strong relationship with Putin, and in a highly unusual move he publically endorsed the candidacy of Medvedev. In an article *"Orthodox Church in unholy alliance with Putin"* (Feb. 23, 2008), the *Daily Telegraph* highlighted the close relationship between the Church and the FSB, commenting on the irony that it was the FSB's predecessor the KGB that led the persecution of clergy during Soviet times. This present and rather unconventional dynamic between Church and state might be explained by a document uncovered from the official Estonian State Archive (record group 131, file 393, pages 125–126) signed by the chairman of the Estonian KGB, Col. I.P. Karpov. This concerns the recruitment into the KGB, on February 28th 1958, of a young priest named Alexis Ridiger. Ridiger was known by the codename *Drozdov.* He was elevated to the post of Patriarch of the Russian Orthodox Church as Alexis II in 1990 after the death of Patriarch Pimen I. Other documentation appears conclusively to support this evidence, as does testimony of former high ranking officials. It seems that the head of the Russian Orthodox Church was indeed an agent of the KGB. Patriarch Alexis passed away in December 2008.

Unlike the EU's political elite, the Russians understand the fact that it is only American economic power and military strength that made the European project possible at all. The Kremlin assumes US hegemony to be in decline, and in much the same way that the West projects its own frameworks onto Russia; it sees an analogy between that decline and the final years of the Soviet experience. Iraq is considered to be *"America's Afghanistan"*. It therefore follows that the EU will be unable to sustain its post-state, post-modernist course without the umbrella of American power. The flaw in this thinking is in assuming that America's setbacks are irreversible. Afghanistan was, at the time, referred to widely as *"Russia's Vietnam"*. It should be remembered that the US survived its painful humiliation in South East Asia, learnt some valuable lessons, and came back as strong as ever.

The political elite of the EU build their credentials by practising compromise. Their Russian counterparts however take pride in their aggressive posturing, and still have the legacy of Marxist dialectics to confound the Europeans in negotiations. Russian negotiating style, like that of the Soviet Union, is about demand and concession: they demand, we concede, they then demand more.

The European Union has attempted to establish a partnership accord with Russia. However, a summit in Helsinki on November 24th 2006 faltered when Poland vetoed the start of the talks in protest at a Russian ban on Polish meat products, which had been imposed in November 2005, and remained in place until December 2008. During the previous year, 2004, imports from Poland and other EU states were suspended in a row over veterinary certificates. The confrontation highlighted two interesting dynamics present in contemporary European politics: Firstly, that within the context of the EU, Poland now feels strong enough to stand up to Russia. Secondly, that Russia still feels confident enough to influence, and exert pressure on, former Soviet states even when they are now EU members.

The proposed partnership accord included provisions on energy, trade and human rights. The European Union, which relies on Russia for one quarter of its gas supplies, wants the pact to include Russian supply guarantees. The consent of all member states is required in order to proceed with the accord, but there are now suggestions of a Russian strategy to divide and destabilise the EU. The *Wall Street Journal* reported that on December 14th 2006, Commission officials registered complaints about Russian efforts to negotiate separate deals to secure meat imports from Eire and Germany. The member states concerned rejected any bilateral deals, and Health Commissioner Markos Kyprianou won assurances from Moscow that an EU-wide ban would not happen. Imports from Poland remained banned at that time, with Russian sources claiming that Poland's food certification system is unreliable and corrupt. There were suggestions of a similar ban on Bulgarian and Romanian meat products. Moscow had suggested at one point that a continent-wide trade agreement on food is impossible. Germany and Denmark are the two main exporters of meat to Russia, accounting for €201.5 million of trade in the first six months of 2006. In 2004, the year before Russia imposed a ban, Poland's exports of meat totalled €40.2 million as against €88 million in 2003, prior to Poland joining the EU.

Talks on a partnership agreement were suspended following the Russian invasion of Georgia, and resumed again in late 2008.

In November 2008, President Sarkozy of France proposed a US-EU-Russia security accord; *"As acting EU council president I propose that mid-2009 we gather for instance within the OSCE [Organisation for Security and Co-operation in Europe] to lay the basis of what might be a future EU security arrangement ...which would of course involve the Russians and the Americans."* In fact, the idea was first put forward by Medvedev, possibly as a vehicle for addressing concerns over the proposed US missile defence shield, which was to be based in Poland and the Czech Republic. France's relationship with Russia is motivated partly by a desire on the part of the former to increase its profile in international relations, and partly by both nations' opposition to American hegemony. In terms of trade, France is not important to Russia, although GDF and Total both have strong links with Gazprom, the latter being involved in development of the Shtockman gas field in the Barents Sea. This will supply gas to Europe through the Nordstream pipeline, with production due to begin in 2013.

"That treaty was the result of the defeat of Russia, and the date of her submission to the continental system. It attacked the honour of the Russians, which some of them were capable of comprehending, and their interest, which all could understand."

So wrote General Count Philippe de Ségur, aide-de-campe to Napoleon Bonaparte during his 1812 expedition to Russia. He referred to the first treaty of Tilsit, agreed between Bonaparte and Tsar Alexander I, following the French victory over the Russian army at Friedland, now known as Pravdinsk, in June 1807. Whilst this treaty created an alliance between the two nations, it effectively placed the Tsar and his armies at the disposal of Bonaparte, a situation as unacceptable to the Russians as was the second treaty of Tilsit to the Prussians, who lost half their territory in the deal. The alliance between France and Russia broke down in 1810, leading eventually to the French invasion of 1812. One cannot help but wonder if this experience influences the way in which Russia views its treaties with Europe to this day, as the relationship between the EU and Russia also seems destined to flounder, due to the basic difference in the approaches of the two polities to the concept of rule of law. The EU seeks peaceful interdependence and security based on law. Russia, however, sees the law merely as an expression of power, and when the power base shifts, or its scope widens, existing laws and agreements can simply be forgotten.

For example; in 2006 Bulgaria was forced to sign an agreement with Gazprom leading to an increase in prices. A deal was already in place, and not due to expire until 2010, but Bulgarian Economy and Energy Minister Rumen Ovcharov warned his government that if it did not acquiesce to Gazprom's demands, Russia was likely to halt gas supplies through Bulgaria. The atrocious hijacking of Sakhalin-2 by Gazprom has already been discussed, and one might ask how Western investors can feel safe when dealing with Russian companies.

Politically, Russia has repeatedly failed the honour commitments made to the Council of Europe (CoE). Following a commitment to enact a moratorium on capital punishment, a prerequisite of CoE membership, the Council revealed on January 28th 1997 that in the first half of the previous year Russian state had executed fifty-three people. Russia had entered into a commitment upon accession to the Council of Europe to put into place a moratorium on executions with effect from the day of accession. These executions clearly constituted a flagrant violation of Russia's commitments and obligations. The fact that in 2002 the Duma passed a motion ending the moratorium shows the contempt that Russia has for international agreements and obligations.

Speaking in the Council on October 2nd 2008 following the Russian action against Georgia, itself a CoE member, Lord Tomlinson stated that, *"The Russian Federation failed to honour the basis of its Council of Europe membership. In so doing, those responsible dishonoured their democracy, their country and themselves. They let us all down and in so doing inflicted a body blow on the Council of Europe's core values."*

Alexander Stubb, Chair of the Organization for Security and Co-operation in Europe (OSCE), speaking on the same matter stated that, *"The recognition of independence for South Ossetia and Abkhazia violates fundamental OSCE principles. As all OSCE participating States, Russia is committed to respecting the sovereignty and territorial integrity of others."*

Membership of the CoE and OSCE are useful baubles for the Kremlin, giving the regime a veneer of respectability, but Russia does not appear to see itself in any way bound by legal obligations it has voluntarily entered into. Ivan Krastev of the Centre for Liberal Strategies writes in *Russia in Global Affairs* (July-Aug 2007) *"Russia is opting for a world in which Kremlin-friendly oligarchs will own English soccer clubs and the Russian middle-class will travel freely all over Europe, but international companies will not be allowed to exploit Russian natural resources, and the Kremlin's domestic critics will be expelled from European capitals".*

Russia seeks a relationship with the EU based on *'asymmetrical interdependence'*, a political concept in which power accrues to the least dependent partner in a relationship.

Actually, this concept is not new, and was a key aspect of Cold War era Soviet political doctrine. The EU is playing perfectly into the hands of the Kremlin, as its component parts, the member states, seek bilateral agreements with Russia in a variety of areas, but most notably in energy. The sale of downstream infrastructure in Western Europe to Russian companies is seemingly offset by Western investment in upstream production processes. There is nothing symmetrical about this exchange of assets, however. With its state-controlled companies controlling distribution in the West, a total Russian monopoly on domestic pipelines and majority stakes in international pipelines coming out of the country, Russia can cut off energy supplies anytime it chooses to do so. Western investment in upstream production facilities is risky, as Sakhalin-2 proved, and the minority holdings of Western companies give Europe no political power whatsoever.

In terms of population, industrial output and military spending (the classic measures of power), the EU outstrips Russia dramatically. Russia's economy, despite its income from oil and gas, remains small. In 2007 Gross Domestic Product was only marginally higher than that recorded for the Benelux countries (source: World Bank). Russia, however, continues to outmanoeuvre its Western counterparts at every twist and turn.

The EU is itself to blame for this extraordinary inversion of power. Its failure to act in a unified manner, with certain member states consistently acting only in their own best interests, means that European relationships with Russia are choreographed by the Kremlin. Economic relationships centre on oil and gas, whilst in the political field the UN veto is wielded as a tool to gain favour or compliance. Russia plays to its strengths, whilst Europe's potential strengths, its size and wealth, are thrown away as the Union languishes in disunity. Even in January 2009, after much posturing from the European Commission over the shutting off of gas supplies through Ukraine, Putin was side-stepping the EU and holding private talks with German Chancellor Angela Merkel in Berlin, and Italian energy giant ENI in Moscow.

Russia's worst case scenario is a Common European Energy Policy. Although European interests are diverse and diffuse, Russian interests are concentrated in a few hands, and primarily in one policy area, energy, and the same clique that runs Russia also owns it.

Its 'Trojan horses' in the EU actively work against such a common policy, with Greece (which receives not only gas but also arms from Russia) and Cyprus (an off-shore haven for Russian-owned businesses) both refusing to support the unbundling of ownership of energy companies in Europe that would weaken Gazprom and other tools of Russian foreign policy. EU member states that try to curry favour with the Kremlin should beware. Vladimir Chizhov, Moscow's ambassador to the EU, and whose son Vasily was expelled from NATO headquarters in April 2009 for spying, stated in an interview with *Capital* magazine, *"Bulgaria is in a good position to become our special partner, a sort of Trojan horse in the EU"*. This did not help Bulgaria when Gazprom turned against them. At a two-day summit on May 21-22, in Khabarovsk, near the border with China, the EU and Russia failed to reach an agreement on an energy pact. Whilst Czech President Vaclav Klaus, whose country then held the rotating EU Presidency, tried to put a positive spin on the failure, Medvedev harshly criticised the EU's attempts to strengthen relationships with former Soviet states such as Ukraine and

Belarus, and thus ensured that the EU continues to speak with 27 voices instead of one. Speaking on Russian TV, he expressed his satisfaction with the *"strategic character of relations"* between the EU and Russia. As already discussed, as recently as June 2009, Romania was seeking to develop its own bilateral energy partnership with the Kremlin.

The EU's strict adherence to legal frameworks and practices place it at a distinct disadvantage, when Russia, as has been illustrated, disregards Western norms, breaks its word and ignores the rules with impunity. How can such a situation be addressed?

Russia cherishes its position in the G8. The other major powers, Canada, France, Germany, Italy, Japan, the United Kingdom and the United States, should be less reticent about devolving decision making back down to the G7, excluding Russia from the process. Suspension from the CoE and OSCE might be considered, given that Russia has consistently broken the commitments made on joining those organisations. Those nations that have flirted with the EU and NATO, such as Georgia and Moldova, have been on the receiving end of Russian trade sanctions. The European Commission might wish to consider assisting those states by fast-tracking them into trade agreements with the EU, opening new and possibly more lucrative markets for their exports. The continuance of the EU-Russia programme may need to be dependent on the observance of the rule of law, and fulfilment of contractual obligations in Russia's dealings with EU member states.

The intention should not be to punish Russia, but to exert pressure on the Kremlin to abide by the same rules as the rest of Europe. Trade agreements that are honoured by one side only or promises that are broken as soon as a shift in power occurs are of no use to the rest of the world, and by accepting these sharp practices the EU is flaunting its weakness and thereby inviting even worse abuses. The fantasies of the 1990s, in which Russia, dependent on Western assistance would gleefully adapt to become a liberal democracy, bound to abide by commercial contracts and international agreements are no longer *realpolitik*.

Alternative fuel strategies for the West.

The only means that Western Europe had of avoiding crisis as a result of the threatened shut-down of natural gas supplies in January 2007 was to stockpile gas. This was a very short-term option, but the only one available. EU energy Commissioner Andris Piebalgs has commented on the importance of Kazakhstan as an alternative supplier to the EU. Whilst the EU negotiates supply contracts, however, China is aggressively buying up Kazakh oil fields. Kazakhstan has also considered withdrawing traditional tax privileges enjoyed by the oil industry, which would lead to significant price increases. Kazakhstan was also involved in negotiations, along with Algeria and Qatar and Uzbekistan, in Russia's planned 'Gas OPEC', a move which could potentially undermine Europe's security of supply. Turkmenistan, a sparsely populated desert region with the second largest gas reserves after Russia, has also signed deals with China, and a pipeline for the import of gas by the latter has been completed.

Great Britain's need to wean itself off of dependency on Russian-supplied energy resources may provide further political motivation for maintaining ownership of the Falkland Islands. The *Falkland Oil and Gas Limited* (FOGL) is an oil and gas exploration company, operating in the undrilled South and East Falkland Basins, potentially a new petroleum province in the South Atlantic. FOGL plans to conduct

ФЕДЕРАЛЬНОЕ СОБРАНИЕ
РОССИЙСКОЙ ФЕДЕРАЦИИ

ГОСУДАРСТВЕННАЯ ДУМА

The author in the Russian State Duma.

further seismic surveys targeting all the leads but with particular emphasis on the approximately 50 most promising. The aim will be to develop 20 high quality, technically sound and potentially economically viable drilling prospects. The Company then intends to develop a multi-well drilling programme. Whilst The Falklands have a mainly agriculturally based economy at present, FOGL believes that the existing infrastructure on the Islands is already capable of supporting the early stages of an oil exploration project.

The latest phase of seismic data acquisition ended on May 5th 2007. The rate of acquisition had recently slowed during periods of poor weather. The total amount of 2D seismic data recorded by FOGL is in the region of 22,450 km.

The main weakness in Putin's energy policy may well turn out to be the inevitable end of the global dependency on fossil fuels. Although the environmentalist's dreams of sustainable and renewable energy sources are far from being realised, the world is looking elsewhere. Nuclear energy is back on the agenda. In Germany, politicians are considering extending the use of nuclear energy beyond 2020, when it is currently planned to terminate nuclear generation. Swedes are now questioning whether they should be bound by the result of 1980 referendum which called for the shutdown of nuclear power stations by 2010. The UK's 12 nuclear power stations supply around 23% of electricity, and with North Sea oil reserves dwindling, Tony Blair placed the question of expansion of the nuclear programme on the agenda at the 2006 Labour Party conference. Interestingly, he cited environmental concerns as one reason to move from fossil fuels to nuclear energy. Both the Conservative Party and the UK

Independence Party have voiced support for nuclear energy. A *French-British Nuclear Forum* was launched in Paris on November 29th 2006 to discuss energy policy and to discuss co-operation in areas including research and long-term security and safety.

The French nuclear energy programme dates back to 1973, and was partly a reaction to events in the Middle East, and partly in acknowledgment of the fact that France had not been particularly blessed in regard to natural resources. From a standing start, France built 56 power stations, and within 15 years was actually exporting energy: a truly remarkable achievement and one that could surely be surpassed with modern technology. This potential renaissance of the European nuclear industry has not gone unnoticed by the Kremlin, of course, and Russia is ensuring its involvement in future projects in the West. In May 2009, Putin personally approved a loan of €3.8 billion, for the construction of the new Belene nuclear power plant in Bulgaria. Russia's nuclear energy monopoly *Atomstroiexport,* which is also involved in Turkish and Iranian nuclear programmes, will be a partner in the project, alongside Belene's two shareholders, Bulgaria's National Electric Company (NEK), and Germany's Rheinisch-Westfälisches Elektrizitätswerk AG (RWE). The German company has already entered into negotiations to sell 50% of its stake to Russian company Inter ROA, a company formed in May 1997 with the purpose of consolidating energy generation and sales in foreign markets. The Russian state own 50% of shares in Inter ROA, and so we are faced with the situation of the Kremlin effectively owning approximately a quarter of the shares in Bulgaria's future "alternative" power source.

There does also remain the highly contentious issue of the disposal of nuclear waste, a sensitive subject in the environmentally conscious EU. The white knight of the East has, however, suggested that Russia may provide a solution by setting aside land for the disposal of imported nuclear waste, thus ensuring Russian fingers are firmly in any future pies. Spent nuclear fuel from Belene is already earmarked for shipping to Russia. The Basle convention on the movement of hazardous waste is riddled with holes, and the potential does exist for Russia to harvest the world's nuclear waste, with all the security problems that may pose, particularly worrying at a time when there are fears about terrorists acquiring nuclear weapons. In June 2009, Medvedev became the first Russian leader to visit Namibia, which produces 10% of the world's uranium. In 2007, an exploration license had been awarded by the Namibian government to a joint venture led by Tekhsabexport, a Russian state firm that sells uranium. More than 40 reactors were being built in 11 countries at this point, and uranium prices had risen substantially on the back of this and the demand for carbon neutral power generation. Control of the sources of Uranium is obviously of great strategic importance, and we would like to think that the European Commission is also making viable contingency plans for the future. During the same tour of Africa, an agreement was also signed on future co-operation in the field of nuclear energy with Nigeria and Namibia.

In terms of renewable energy sources, the EU has committed its members to ambitious targets. In March 2007, European leaders agreed to a binding EU-wide target to source 20% of their energy needs from renewable sources such as biomass, hydro, wind and solar power by 2020. On 23 January 2008, the Commission put forward differentiated targets for each individual member state, based on the per capita GDP of each country. However, in early 2009 the Commission admitted that the first rung, 12% by 2010, was unlikely to be achieved. Member states proceed at different paces, with Germany having already exceeded its targets. Denmark has taken the lead in wind energy production, and approximately 27% of the country's energy came from renewable sources by 2009. The Danish Wind Industry Association reported that in 2008, wind power technology exports earned the country €5.7 billion, some 7.2% of Denmark's total exports in that year. Other member states lag behind, however, with seven countries actually having a lower renewables mix that they did in 2004.

chapter 6
the medvedev cabinet: a new doctrine, or a holding action?

Forbidden by Article 81 of the Russian constitution from a third consecutive Presidential term, Putin left his office in the hands of Dmitry Medvedev, his protégé from the St Petersburg days, a former deputy prime minister, and chairman of Gazprom.

Medvedev is widely seen as little more than a puppet-cum-caretaker for Vladimir Putin, as the latter fulfils his legal obligations by stepping down from the Presidency, if only temporarily. But if Medvedev is truly in charge, then what kind of a President is he, and how does his administration compare to that of Putin? In terms of his personnel and his political pronouncements, he might be seen as confused and contradictory.

Medvedev lambasts the US for interfering outside its own borders, whilst at the same time claiming Russia's *"privileged interests"* in its own neighbourhood. He has attacked the US for its military relationship with Georgia, actually laying the blame for the war on the White House, whilst Russia actively arms Venezuela and other South American states. In recognising the breakaway regions of South Ossetia and Abkhazia, Russia assumes the right to swallow up existing nation states and to create new ones.

He blames the US for imposing upon the world financial policy and practice that has led to the credit crunch, whilst demanding a more proactive role for the near bankrupt Russia in world affairs.

In his proclamation that Russian people should be able to take *"a more active role in the country's political life"* he suggests a more pluralistic polity, but his commitment to liberal values should assuage fears of a return to Marxist theory. The concept of "sovereign democracy", however, embraced by many of those advisors close to the Presidency, indicates that the concept of the political project is alive and well in Russia. Sovereign democracy counters the Anglo-Saxon model of liberal democracy, in that it places the interests of the individual below those of the state, holding that whilst the state has supreme power, as the state belongs to the people, then the polity is democratic. Medvedev himself has actually criticised the theory of sovereign democracy. Some observers believe that the European Union may adapt to this Russian model at some time in the future, although such a shift in doctrine could only take place if the EU finalises its borders both geographically and ideologically, something which is highly unlikely to ever happen. One might also ask if sovereign democracy and postmodernism are mutually exclusive.

In terms of the more senior government appointments, there is some scepticism as to how much input Medvedev has actually had, at least in the earliest months of his presidency, compared with his predecessor. Certainly the cabinet was loaded with pro-Putin personnel.

Arkady Dvorkovitch, for example, was a key aide to Putin, and was responsible for the 13% flat tax initiative that proved so successful in raising tax revenue, historically a major problem in Russia, where the state competes with organised crime for tribute. Educated at Duke University in North Carolina USA, and Moscow State University, and an expert in public finance, he has consistently advocated tax reductions. The young economist is taken very seriously in international circles. He has worked for the government since 1994, when he joined the Economic Expert Group in Moscow, a think tank that advises the Russian Finance Ministry, rising to the post of director in 1997. From 2001 until 2004, Dvorkovitch was Deputy Minister of Economic Development and Trade of the Russia, and was appointed Head of the Presidential Experts Directorate of the President Executive Office in April 2004. In 2005 he was appointed to the board of "Svyazinvest", which controls numerous telecom enterprises in Russia, to oversee the Kremlin's interests. The company was created by Presidential decree in 1994, with the state seeking overseas investment, but privatisation was never successfully achieved, and by 2009 talk was of full re-nationalisation. He is now the Russian *"Sherpa"* in the G8, and occupies Leonid Brezhnev's former offices in Staraya Ploshchad.

Another key Putin ally is Sergei Naryshkin, a former deputy Prime Minister. He was named head of Medvedev's Kremlin administration as Chief of Staff of the Presidential Executive Office. An engineer and economist, Naryshkin was reputedly trained alongside Putin at the "Andropov Red Banner Institute", formerly known as School No. 101 of the KGB First Main Directorate, and which specialises in foreign intelligence. In 1982 he served as an economics advisor in the Soviet embassy in Belgium, although his role was widely believed to have more to do with his KGB credentials. In the 1990s, like Dmitry Medvedev, he was involved in governance in St Petersburg at the same time as Vladimir Putin.

Naryshkin's deputy is Vladislav Yuryevich Surkov, who is believed to have contributed to Putin's 2004 election victory, and is also reputed to have been involved in the Nashi movement. Another economist, he is a prominent advocate of the concept of sovereign democracy, Russia's alternative model to Western liberal democracy.

Below Surkov, Alexander Dmitryevich Beglov, Deputy Chief of Staff of the Presidential Executive Office is another much trusted former colleague of Putin's from his St Petersburg days. There is no suggestion that Beglov, unlike so many of Putin's allies, is connected with the KGB/FSB. Surkov shares his job title with Alexei Alexeyevich Gromov, a former diplomat whose background in the Soviet Ministry of Foreign Affairs might hint at KGB connections.

Possibly the most interesting appointment of all is that of Sergei Ivanov. When he was placed in the office of First Deputy Minister in 2005, having served four years as defence minister - the first civilian to hold that post - it was widely speculated that he was being groomed to succeed Putin. He was subsequently relieved of his defence portfolio in 2007 and appointed First Deputy Prime Minister. Ivanov is another graduate of the Red Banner Institute, and also studied at the Leningrad (now St Petersburg) State University at the same time as Putin. Both men trained at the Higher KGB School in Minsk, and served together in the same KGB directorate in Leningrad. Eventually he became Deputy Director of the FSB under Putin.

The Leningrad/St Petersburg connection takes an interesting twist when one considers Putin's role as Deputy Mayor from 1994–96. The Mayor at the time was Anatoly Sobchak, regarded by many as being one of the key architects of, and driving force behind, the Russian democratisation process that was sadly to fail under his own

Dmitry Anatolyevich Medvedev, third President of the Russian Federation.
Photo: Courtesy of www.kremlin.ru

protégé. Previously, in 1990, Putin had been appointed as an advisor on International relations to Sobchak and subsequently became head of the committee for external relations. It is interesting to note that in his political autobiography, *For a new Russia* (1992), Sobchak does not mention Putin's name even once. Putin had actually studied under Sobchak at Leningrad State University, and after the latter died in Kaliningrad in 2000, the *New York Times* described him in an obituary as *"Mentor to Putin"*.

So what of Medvedev?

Medvedev has taken pains to avoid appearing weaker than Putin, and the attack on Georgia helped his image in Russia. It is notable, however, that in a break with Russian political tradition, he initially avoided direct criticism of his predecessor, and seemed intent on building on, rather than replacing, Putin's policies. His programme appears ambitious, with Russia's plans for a moon landing proceeding, and the structural reorganisation of the military announced by Putin continuing apace. In March 2009 he announced a major overhaul of Russia's nuclear arsenal, beginning in 2011, at a time when Western powers are proactively seeking to reduce the number of warheads being held, and are scaling down their deterrents in the assumption that Cold War fears are now redundant. To make such an announcement at a time when US support for Ukrainian and Georgian membership of NATO is softening, and the proposed missile shield based on Polish and Czech soil is floundering, might be considered counter productive, or even provocative. A brief war was fought in 2008 partly to underline Russian concerns in those areas, and indelicate and badly timed proclamations on rearmament may jeopardise the political gains that were made at that time.

To many Western observers Medvedev does appear somewhat weak, and the Western media remains far more interested in Putin. His performance at the crucial G20 summit in London in April 2009 did nothing to enhance his image overseas. His summary of the meeting was somewhat melancholic. *"I would like to say that this is a turning point... but as a responsible man I cannot say this,"* he said. Prior to the summit, Medvedev had held his first meeting with US President Obama. After a 70-minute meeting, the two leaders announced a number of agreements, pledging co-operation on various foreign policy issues. Possibly the most interesting was the agreement to renegotiate the Strategic Arms Reduction Treaty (START), with Obama leading the call for reductions in warheads held globally. Medvedev's willingness to go along with this appeared somewhat to contradict his earlier proclamations on the rebuilding of Russia's nuclear forces. Cynics might speculate that he sees the opportunity to cadge some foreign money to pay for the decommissioning of some of Russia's dangerously obsolete nuclear arsenal.

Medvedev has acknowledged that the US and Russia had diverged somewhat in a number of policy objectives during the time of the Putin/Bush administrations, leading to speculation that he may be seeking to find common ground on policy with the Obama administration. Many observers believe that Putin regarded Bush as naive, and possessing little understanding of the dynamics of international relations. These weaknesses, perceived or real, would have given no incentive whatsoever for the Russian leader to position himself closely to the Bush administration. The latter's comment about looking into Putin's eyes and "seeing his soul" was simply laughed at. Soviet dissident Vladimir Bukovsky commented afterwards that, *"In my many encounters with KGB officers soul is the one thing I failed to spot."* In a letter to President Bush in 2003, Bukovsky and Elena Bonner, widow of Andrei Sakharov, wrote of the Putin regime, *"... the KGB has won. After ten years of some hesitant, half-hearted attempts at reform, the power was handed back to them, once again, and they were very quick to re-establish their authority throughout the country, as well as to reinstate the old symbols of the Soviet Union - the national anthem and the Red flag in the Army. The last outlets of independent media were closed down one by one. We did not have political prisoners for ten years; we have them now... Corruption today in Russia is something out of the other world. It is not a corruption anymore; it is a system where the KGB (now called FSB) is running most of the organised crime, protection racket, drug trafficking, arms sales and contract killings."*

Russians themselves are sceptical about the extent of Medvedev's power. In a survey by the Levada Centre polling group in early 2009, only 12% of those polled believed that he was really running the country. 34% believed that Putin was still running Russia from the office of Prime Minister. Interestingly, when asked to name politicians they trusted, 36% named Medvedev, whilst 48% named Putin.

Nevertheless, it might be premature to write Medvedev off as a puppet. His appointment of Igor Shuvalov as First Deputy Prime Minister, working under Putin, is interesting. Shuvalov, an economic liberal, is an acknowledged defender of shareholder's rights. This appointment might be seen as reassuring by some Western investors, although it should be remembered that Shuvalov was hawkish on the matter of the proposed US missile defence, saying in 2007, *"The Russian people, all the people, all the generations would never easily accept the deployment of that equipment along Russian borders..."* Alexei Kudrin and Arkady Dvorkovitch mentioned previously, both have records of defending liberal economic practice and opposing nationalisation.

In May 2009, during a visit to the city of Kirov, Medvedev announced a timetable for implementation of a plan to pay the equivalent of 12 months' unemployment benefit to people wishing to start small businesses. The plan quickly garnered support from the Ministries of Health and Social Development, and Economic Development as well as a host of regional administrations. This is particularly interesting, as it may be seen as a way of quickly achieving a degree of the diversification that is chronically lacking in the Russian economy. One might compare this initiative with the Italian economy, which is dominated by small and medium sized family-owned businesses. It is this slightly eccentric economic model that is credited with helping Italy to weather previous storms, such as that precipitated by the 1973 oil crisis. Medvedev's plan may provide roots for recovery, although traditional problems of tax collection may be exacerbated if the newly created enterprises are allowed to join Russia's grey economy. This problem has been alleviated considerably since the implementation of the Russian Tax Code, which began in 1998, and Putin's introduction of a 13% flat rate tax which increased income tax revenue by an impressive 47%.

Since his inauguration, Medvedev has consistently spoken out about the *"social evil"* of corruption, which the Russian legal system has failed to eradicate. *"Corruption as a social evil is always dangerous,"* he has said. *"As applied to the justice system, it is exceptionally dangerous ... It seems that current legislation should reliably protect judicial independence, but pressure and influence are exerted, administrative resources are employed and direct bribery is often used."* He acknowledged the fact that many Russians seeking justice have turned to the European Court of Human Rights, given their lack of trust in their own country's legal system. Since 1998, Russians have filed something in the region of 46,000 cases with the ECHR, representing almost 20% of the court's total caseload.

In May 2008 Medvedev had established the Presidential Council for Combating Corruption, with himself as its head. The Council's main tasks are to prepare proposals for the President on formulating and implementing anti-corruption policy, coordinating anti-corruption work by the executive authorities at the different levels of governance, and monitoring implementation of the measures set out in the National Anti-Corruption Plan. Medvedev gave the Council just one month to prepare the plan; he clearly recognises the importance of being perceived as being equally as decisive as his predecessor.

The proposed plan contains four sections:

The first provides for legislative provisions to combat corruption. This is a very important section as it defines *corruption*, a practical component of the fight against this problem. It also introduces the requirements and obligations for people working in the public sector, including the courts. It includes a number of proposals for the prevention of corruption and the provision of equal access to the due process of law as well as a number of new legislative concepts connected with bringing into line the current legislature with several international conventions.

The second section covers the streamlining of governmental administration. This is mostly a set of improvements in the daily practices and routines of civil servants, in which opportunities for corruption often arise. It is proposed to introduce regulations in respect to property use and to improve rules of government procurement. It is proposed to devolve certain functions of federal government agencies to regions or to the private sector, as well as to improve the monitoring procedure including via civil society mechanisms. Serious attention is proposed to be directed to the measures to prevent conflicts of interest among civil servants.

The third section covers legal education and training of legal personnel. It is proposed actively to use the media as well as non-governmental organizations in the fight against corruption. The qualifications of lawyers are also to be improved.

The fourth and final section introduces a set of top-priority measures for the implementation of the plan.

In March 2009 Medvedev signed a decree aimed at reforming the civil service, again with the intention of fighting corruption. Medvedev's plans in this respect are ambitious and far reaching - possibly too much so to be realistically viable. They do, however, address many of the obstacles to any future democratisation. A legal definition of corruption is long overdue, and the institutionalisation of the concept of equal access to the law is a prerequisite for any state aspiring to democratic credentials.

Dmitry Medvedev: Putting Russia on centre stage.
Photo courtesy of: www.kremlin.ru

Medvedev on the environment.

It is worth discussing Medvedev's attitude to environmental issues. Shortly after taking office, at a meeting in the Kremlin in June 2008, the new President called for higher standards of environmental protection and for the state to finance renewable energy projects. In a rare comment on ecological concerns in Russia's rapid-growth economy, he was quoted by news agency *Interfax* as saying *"If we think only of the energy wasted in our heating networks, our country is first in the world: It is a bad record...with respect to energy efficiency, the majority of manufacturers lag behind modern times."* After decades of Soviet neglect, Russia has more than its share of environmental degradation and recent economic growth has exacerbated the situation considerably. Medvedev referred to the fact that one million Russians live in environments that have *"dangerous levels of pollution,"* while experts say two-thirds of Russia's 142 million citizens have access to drinking water that is below international standards for pollution levels. He also made reference to the draft of a proposed bill on permissible levels of industrial emissions, scheduled to be tabled in the State Duma later that year. Russia ratified the Kyoto Treaty in November 2004, partly as a move to gain EU support for Russian entry into the WTO.

In June 2009 Medvedev set greenhouse gas emission goals, saying that Russia, the world's third largest emitter of greenhouse gases, would aim to cut its emissions by 30 billion tonnes between 1990 and 2020. This target has, however, as its base line, the 1990 figures for the Soviet Union as a whole and not just Russia. In reality, this means that Medvedev's "cuts" will actually allow for a 30%

increase in emissions. The targets mean cumulative cuts of 30 billion tonnes of greenhouse gases from 1990 (Soviet Union) levels, which implies that Russia will emit about 3 billion tonnes of greenhouse gas in 2020 compared with 2.2 billion tonnes in 2007.

Whilst this angered environmentalists, and will have disheartened other nations genuinely seeking to cut emissions, Russia should be seen in the context of a developing economy. We should remember that despite its vast size, Russia has a small economy, roughly comparable to that of the Benelux countries. There is a valid argument put forward by developing nations concerning environmental responsibility. They will point out that the West has achieved much of its growth at a time when such concerns were not to the fore, and that we have devastated vast swathes of the planet, pumped carbon into the atmosphere for decades, and left our own oceans virtually sterile. Emerging nations might ask why they should be subject to stringent environmental checks that will hamper their own development while the West enriched itself with scarcely a thought for the well-being of the planet. In many cases, although this might not strictly apply to Russia with its highly developed technical capabilities, developing nations simply cannot afford the expensive technologies required to bring their industries up to Western standards.

As an adjunct to the Montreal Protocol (1990), which successfully reduced the emission of CFCs and other ozone depleting substances, the Multilateral Fund for the Montreal Protocol was established, whereby developing economies received financial assistance in implementing the protocol. Without this fund, it is highly unlikely that China or India, for example, could have ratified. Whilst it may not be possible to repeat such a scheme in other areas, there needs to be an understanding of the different levels of development, and the problems that many nations will face in meeting the same standards as the West. It is also worth noting that despite the success of Montreal, Russia has stood out amongst the global community for its non-compliance. Not eligible for financial assistance from the Multilateral Fund, Russia turned to the Global Environment Facility (GEF), a joint venture of the United Nations Development Programme (UNDP), the United Nations Environment Programme (UNEP), and the World Bank, which was established to provide funds for developing countries to implement environmental projects. Total funding of $78.8 million was provided through the World Bank between 1997 and 2001. Russia's acceptance of Montreal was of great importance, as it had traditionally been one of the world's largest producers and consumers of ozone-depleting substances and the sole producer of ozone-depleting substances among the countries of the former Soviet Union. In 1990, when production peaked, the nation manufactured an estimated 198,000 metric tonnes, accounting for between 15 and 20 percent of world production.

In its decision XIII/17 of the United Nations Environmental Programme heavily criticised Russia for its performance up to 2000, although it did "*note with appreciation the fact that the Russian Federation closed CFC production as from 20 December 2000 and stopped Annex A and B ODS import and export operations as from 1 March 2000, as was confirmed in the letter of the Prime Minister of the Russian Federation of 9 December 2000 and of the First Deputy Minister of Natural Resources of the Russian Federation of*

9 October 2000." In that same year, however, Russia was alleged to be the source of much of the illegal CFCs coming onto the international market. Again, Russia was demonstrating its total disregard for legal obligations it had voluntarily entered into. Medvedev's greenhouse gas emissions targets suggest that nothing has changed and cynics might wonder if Russian ratification of Kyoto might have more to do with the opportunity to sell lucrative *carbon credits.* In fact, in 2007 Gazprom announced its intention to sell carbon dioxide emissions credits needed in order to burn all that gas it sells to Europe. In this venture, Gazprom will be competing with commodity traders and others, but its position as a state company will give it an edge over the competition.

Financial crisis.

The Governor of Russia's Central Bank, Sergei Ignatyev and Finance Minister Alexei Kudrin were summoned to the Duma on November 19 2008 to explain their strategy for weathering the global financial crisis, which had been growing in scale since mid-2007.

Russians were scandalised to learn that Russia's international reserves had been deposited abroad. Ignatyev and Kudrin assured the parliamentarians that this is the surest way of protecting national assets. Interestingly, the Central Bank has been ditching dollars and investing in the Euro and other European securities.

What was the most alarming revelation, however, is the news that between August and mid-November 2008, Russia had seen its foreign reserves dwindle by 24% as the Kremlin struggled to prop up the Rouble. In September and October alone, £57.5 billion was spent in this way, although ordinary

Russians were unconvinced, and showed their concerns by emulating the Central Bank, and buying up foreign currency. Ignatyev dropped a further bombshell when he announced that he expected inflation to be 13–14% in 2008, way above the government target.

The World Bank shared the governor's pessimism, and lowered its forecast for growth of Russian GDP in 2009 from 6.5% to 3%. Unemployment was expected to rise moderately, to around 6%. Economics Minister Elvira Nabiullina called for a "new economic model", recognising the need for diversification of economic activity. But with cheap credit a mere memory, falling oil prices and the spectre of inflation, which has caused so much political chaos in Russia in the past, it may be too little too late. At the beginning of October 2008, Ignatyev had announced the imminent bankruptcy of 50 to 70 banks. In actual fact, by the end of November the regulator had shut down only nine banks.

A survey by Ernst & Young, leaked to the Russian press in November, revealed that 113 of their clients had laid off 8% of managerial staff, and 6% of lower level workers. On December 1st 2008, TNK-BP, the Anglo-Russian oil company announced the layoff of 390 management staff and the withdrawal of 200 vacancies. This represents a cutback of 19% of its total staff and follows the loss of 148 technical staff in April of this year. This group has been enmired in controversy, as the controlling oligarchs sought to squeeze out their British partners and take control of the venture, and chief executive Robert Dudley also formally stepped down from his position, to be temporarily replaced by Tim Summers before the oligarch's planned chosen one, Denis Morozov, could be annointed. Eventually, it was Mikhail

Fridman, a young oligarch not unaccustomed to making money under controversial circumstances, who was appointed interim CEO in May 2009. Fridman was the founder, in 1988, of the company *Alfa-Eco.* This became the *Alfa Group Consortium,* one of Russia's largest privately owned business conglomerates, and a part owner of TNK-BP.

The layoffs were blamed on falling oil prices: Oil fell from a record high of $147 a barrel in July 2008 to little more than $40 a barrel by December 2008. It subsequently emerged that in mid-November Siberian oil was being traded on the domestic market at $10 a barrel. A BP spokesman confirmed that from October, Russia had been trading oil at a loss. Output was down by 6%, and leading producers, including Tatneft and Rosneft, the biggest Russian oil producer, were likely to cancel tanker exports from Black Sea ports due to the heavy export tariffs imposed by the Russian government. This taxation represented a major source of income for the Russian state, and whilst tariffs were cut from a high of $51, they remained at a crippling $40 a barrel.

Despite the fact that tank output reached its highest level since the cold war in 2008, the highly important defence industry has been particularly hard hit by the crisis, as so many of its customers are the oil and gas rich states that Russia seeks to cement new strategic relationships with. All have been hit by falling prices, and historical data points to a correlation between the price of oil and the volume of the global trade in weapons: during periods of high oil prices, the demand for weapons increases, and vice-versa. Now, the weak price structure is likely to lead to fewer and smaller defence orders from developing countries. Whilst there is probably no threat of cancellation of the Algerian, Venezuelan and Iranian orders already secured by Rosoboronexport, new orders from other oil producing states may be harder to secure. Increasing metal prices, led by Chinese economic growth, have increased the production costs of armaments, and domestically there may also be an impact on the defence industry as according to the Russian Statistical Service 38.6% of the production of Russia's defence plants goes to civilian customers. This sector has been hit by all aspects of the economic crisis.

Putin and Medvedev appeared divided on what to do: Putin favoured aggressive nationalisation of companies, such as the cement and aluminium plants owned by one-time Kremlin favourite and formerly Russia's richest man, Oleg Deripaska. Medvedev expressed the opposite view, stating that whilst state ownership might serve as a temporary anti-crisis tool, eventual privatisation should be the aim. *"The government,"* said Arkady Dvorkovitch, the president's chief economic adviser, *"cannot replace the private sector, the market, and business, nor is it going to do so."*

Whilst Europe and the US reacted to the global crisis by flirting with protectionism and economic nationalism, Russia, like China, recognised the opportunity for a shift in the balance of international power. Medvedev declared ahead of the November 2008 summit of the Asia-Pacific Economic Co-operation forum in Peru that the emerging economies should, *"...assume the task to unravel the world economic crisis"*. These economies could, he suggested, *"become leaders in the post-crisis period."* Russia's growing strategic relationship with China may be beneficial in this context.

conclusion

In the opening paragraph of this book, I referred to Vladimir Bukovsky. This gentleman, who I am very privileged to know, spent 12 years of his life in prisons, labour camps, and in the *Psikhushka,* so-called hospitals where inmates underwent forced psychiatric treatment in order to cure them of their opposition to the communist regime. Bukovsky has done more than any other to expose this practice. According to Anne Applebaum's, *Gulag: A History*, (Doubleday, 2003) at least 365 dissidents were treated for *"politically defined madness",* and forced to endure unspeakable horrors including restraint, electric shocks, electromagnetic torture, radiation torture, entrapment, servitude, and treatment with a range of drugs. There are possibly hundreds more who are forgotten, or whose cases were not officially documented. Viktor Aleksandrovich Nekipelov, the Russian poet and human rights campaigner who, like Bukovsky, was a veteran of the Psikhushka, referred to the doctors in these institutions as, *"no better than the criminal doctors who performed inhuman experiments on the prisoners in Nazi concentration camps".* The Soviet concentration camp network, the *Gulag,* although very different to the Nazi system, was equally heinous, and although its primary *raison d'être* was not extermination, the results were too often the same, and the system killed millions, many of whom were forcibly deported during the Stalinist era. As many as 30,000 British and Commonwealth soldiers, "liberated" by the Soviets from German POW camps also ended their days in the Gulag. The book *Soldiers of Misfortune: Washington's Secret Betrayal of American POWs in the Soviet Union* by James D. Sanders, Mark A. Sauter, and R. Cort Kirkwood (1992) claimed that 20,000 US servicemen were also taken by the Soviets, and that *"Starting in 1945, the Soviet Union became the second-largest employer of American servicemen in the world."* A US Department of Defence press release, dated 09 Dec 2003, revealed that Deputy Assistant Secretary of Defense Jerry Jennings had visited Moscow as part of the work of a joint U.S.-Russia commission set up in 1992 to explore the question of whether Americans were held in, or transported through, the former Soviet Union during WWII, the Cold War, the Korean War and the Vietnam War. The cases of more than 200 airmen who went missing during the Korean War were discussed. It is widely held that downed American fliers, especially electronic warfare officers, were routinely sent to Moscow for interrogation and execution. It should be pointed out that during the period of the Yeltsin government, Moscow began to open its files, and US investigators were given access to these, and to Russian veterans.

Although the Gulag was officially disbanded in the 1960s, so-called *free-labour camps* remain in operation in Siberia, as a part of the Russian penal system, to this day, accommodating up to one million inmates. The Russians have a word - *"etapirovanie"* - which means "transport in stages". In 2005, Valerii Abramkin, head of the Moscow Centre for Prison Reform, was quoted in the *Moscow Times* as saying the time during which prisoners are in transit is used *to "shock them and break their spirit."* Unable to communicate with the outside world, with up to 20 prisoners in a six-berth compartment, they are at the mercy of their guards. Abramkin told the newspaper that during stops, prisoners are often pulled out and made to lie down or kneel in the snow or dirt for hours while being beaten. A Labour camp in the far northern Yamal Peninsula, near the Arctic Circle, also remains in service, and it was rumoured that Mikhail Khordokovsky, the oligarch who fell out with the Kremlin after he sponsored pro-democratic political parties, has served part of his sentence there. Relatives have the right to know where loved ones are incarcerated, but there is no time-frame laid down within which this information must be imparted, so in reality many prisoners simply disappear into the system. Traditionally, NGOs would fight for the rights of such individuals, but Putin has shut many of these down, of course....

As recently as 2001, the *St Petersburg Times* reported that North Korea was sending prisoners to Siberian Labour camps as a means of paying off its Soviet-era debt to Russia.

A Russian observer might point, quite fairly and reasonably, to the murderous excesses of the British in South Africa, where our concentration camps and the atrocities committed against Boer civilians predated the horrors of Hitler and Stalin. I would accept such points, as I would accept that the treatment of the indigenous people of Kenya during the Mau Mau uprising was almost on a par with the deeds of the Nazi and Red armies, albeit on a far smaller scale. We are not innocent, and our own history is littered with atrocities. Sadly, Russia still appears to be stuck in that phase of its development.

If we criticise the Kremlin for the way in which Gazprom, and the energy sector in general, is used as a tool of Russian foreign and economic policy, how can we possibly defend the past activities of exploitative organisations as the East

India, or Hudson Bay Companies, on which much of Britain's wealth was built?

Medvedev's law banning certain interpretations of Soviet history to be discussed publically causes a sharp intake of breath amongst historians, instinctively wary of any form of censorship. But we should remember that more than a dozen European countries have laws that ban 'denial' of the Holocaust. Certain Western nations wallow in nostalgia over the Second World War, so why should not Russia try to protect the memory of its vast numbers of casualties? We might well argue that this law is abusing that memory as a smokescreen for the horrors of Stalinism, and that the dictator's bungling approach to foreign policy and incompetent handling of the war effort probably contributed more than almost any other factor to his country's suffering; but one could equally argue that those countries that have enacted Holocaust denial laws are simply wracked with guilt about their own collaboration with the Nazis, and are seeking to make amends to the victims.

NATO's attack on Belgrade in 1999 exposed Russia's weakness through its inability to prevent the action either politically or militarily. It was almost inevitable that a show of strength in order to restore national pride would be on the political agenda, so we might say that the political seeds of the Georgian crisis were sown nine years earlier in Serbia. We criticise Russia's subsequent recognition of the Georgian breakaway states of South Ossetia and Abkhazia, whilst accepting almost without question or comment the West's recognition of Kosovo, almost as if we have some God-given infallibility that gives us alone the right to bestow nationhood.

As previously stated, Russia is at a different stage in its development, and in any case cannot realistically be expected to conform to Western norms. Post-Soviet Russia is also charting its course based on the dynamics between itself and its neighbours, many of which are Asian countries which have shared historic experiences with the Russian people. These relationships are every bit as important to Russia as its relationships with Western Europe and the US. Its political outlook is, accordingly, very different to our own, and the assumption that is still held by many Western observers - namely that Russia will develop into a liberal democracy in our own mould - is completely absurd.

The political incompatibility of East and West is not the real source of confrontation: the lack of understanding that results from it is. The issues that lead to break down of trust, failure to honour treaties, etc, are mere details. America's perceptions of its own hegemony, now faded and jaded, but clung to stubbornly, and Europe's post-state mindset, are at complete odds with Russian sovereign democracy. Russia has adjusted from communism to pseudo liberal democracy and then to sovereign democracy in just two decades. It has, out of necessity, made enormous changes, political, social, and economic, in order to allow it to engage with the rest of the world. The West needs to reciprocate: our political institutions, national and trans-national, may need to be adjusted or realigned to take account of Russia's place in our increasingly globalised world. Trans-national governance is a fact of life in many policy areas, and we will find our concerns and requirements overlapping more and more with those of Russia in the near future. Institutions and policies must reflect this. In order to understand the Russian phenomenon it is important that we are able to transcend our own epistemology, abandon our Cold War mindset, and accept that whilst our own liberal democratic model may serve us well, it is not for everybody. If we cannot accommodate or even understand Russia, how will we cope with China in a few years time?

As impenetrable as the Russian mindset is to us, it is important to try to at least understand how they see our actions. Ruslan Pukhov, Director of Moscow's of Centre for Analysis of Strategies and Technologies (CAST) wrote in the 'Moscow Defense Brief' (#1 (15) 2009) *"...the salient lesson of the August conflict in Georgia is that Russian public opinion was completely shocked by the fervent, anti-Russian reaction of the West to what happened, and by the readiness of Western countries to support and justify any and all anti-Russian actions, including direct and undisguised attack on peacekeeping zones and peacekeeping forces, the killing of Russian peacekeepers and Russian citizens. In effect, the West has denied Russia any right to self-defence in principle. This made an unexpectedly big impression on Russia, and deeply troubled Russian public opinion across the political spectrum. This resulted in a significant surge of anti-Western sentiment in Russia, and a massive rise of hostility towards military and political cooperation with the West, especially with the USA. The implications of this growth of anti-Western sentiment have not yet been fully appreciated."* This is, of course, completely at odds with our own interpretation of events, which holds that Russia had bestowed citizenship on Russian speaking Georgian citizens, and then created a crisis so that it might intervene militarily in order to defend the interests of those "Russian" citizens. Western observers will instinctively accept that Georgia acted in a way that reflects our own determination to defend democratic principles. However, these are *western* democratic principles, and they differ from those of Russia, and quite probably from those of the Georgian political elite, who may simply have seen in this crisis an opportunity to further their own interests. The truth is likely to lie somewhere between the two accounts.

It has been widely assumed that Putin will run for the Presidency in 2012. He is, however, in a slightly disadvantageous position as Prime Minister, as he shoulders the responsibility for the economy. With falling fuel prices set against the background of an international economic crisis and the Russian stock market losing 80% of its value at one point, he is vulnerable. On the other hand, Medvedev, as President, is cushioned from blame. We can present evidence to support the argument that Medvedev is merely keeping Putin's chair warm, but we can just as easily point to reforms and actions that suggest Medvedevism is real, that he is ploughing his own furrow, but that he is pragmatic and brave enough to acknowledge and to continue with Putin's more successful policies. On a visit to Japan in May 2009, Putin gave a strong insight into his intentions. The outcome of the economic crisis would determine which of the two men stood in 2012. *"I have known him* (Medvedev) *for a long time and I know he will look at his political future based on the interests of the country,"* he said.

The coincidence of Medvedev and Obama taking their respective offices within months of one another may hold significance for future relations. Speaking to the Italian newspaper *Corriere della Sera* in early July 2009, the

Russian President made the point of referring to his American counterpart, at the beginning of the interview, as his *"colleague"*. He acknowledged the need to address a number of issues such as inter-regional conflicts, and spoke of his desire to see stronger trading ties between the two nations. Most interestingly of all, in the context of a forthcoming G8 summit, he appeared to defer to the G5 (France, Germany, Japan, the United Kingdom, and the United States) in setting the agenda for the meeting. On other issues including Iran and Korea he appeared signal his willingness for some convergence on international policy. There may be an opening for greater progress in east-west relations now, than even at the dawn of the Yeltsin era.

Medvedev has repeatedly pointed out that he, as President, is in charge, and that the Prime Minister is responsible for matters economic. This has often occurred in the context of discussion of the global economic crisis. A strong advocate of a new global reserve currency, however, he has emphasised that even in this area, long term strategy is in his domain. This is a policy also being pushed by Beijing: a fact that we may imbue with great significance.

In Vienna, in 1961, at their one Presidential meeting, the young John F. Kennedy was overwhelmed and humiliated by Soviet Premier Nikita Khrushchev. He was lambasted for his lack of support for states seeking to free themselves from the grip of the colonial powers, and strongly warned about the folly of surrounding the Soviet Union with military bases. The US president had been warned by his advisors against the meeting, and immediately afterwards, Paul Nitze, the US assistant Secretary of

Defence, described the meeting as *"just a disaster"*. The President's poor performance and perceived weaknesses were to have dire consequences: within months Khrushchev ordered work to begin on the Berlin wall, and the deployment of missiles to Cuba in 1962 brought the world to the brink of war.

With this debacle in mind, President George W. Bush, speaking to the Knesset in May 2008 warned against negotiating with America's adversaries, describing such a process as "appeasement". The events of 1961 must have also been in the thoughts of another young President, Barack Obama, when he arrived in Moscow for his own first meeting with the Russian leadership in April 2009.

US-Russia relations were generally agreed to have sunk to their lowest ebb since the Cold war during the final years of the Bush Presidency. His adversarial cold war mindset, however, contrasts strongly with that of Obama, who since taking office has vowed to improve the relationship. His opposite number, Medvedev, also appears to have adopted a different stance to his own predecessor.

Indeed, whilst Obama took time for a breakfast meeting with Putin at his dacha, he has described him, just days before, as *"having one foot in the old way of doing business and one foot in the new"*. Obama stated confidently that it was time to move forward, and that Medvedev *"understands that"*. The signal could not be stronger - Obama can, and will, do business with Medvedev.

The meeting of the two men resulted in the highly significant agreement on the progression of the replacement of the START arms treaty, which dates from 1991. A legally binding treaty was intended to be concluded by the end of 2009. Agreements were also reached on Afghanistan and Iran, although it the latter case it is in Russia's strategic interests to keep that country isolated from the west, thus keeping Europe dependent on gas, which Iran possesses massive reserves. If the price of this is a nuclear armed Iran, then let us be under no illusions: the Kremlin can easily live with that if it has to. Two highly significant concessions from the Russians were support for US/UN position on North Korea, and an agreement to allow the transit of US troops and military equipment through Russia en route to Afghanistan.

It was highly reassuring that despite Obama's refusal to link the proposed missile defence shield to the talks, or to compromise his position on Georgian sovereignty, Medvedev felt able to proceed. This surprised many observers. Putin, however, speaking to the Moscow News three days before the summit, was unable to move away from the issues, stating that *"If we see something new, if our American partners abandon, for example, building new military complexes in Europe, abandon plans for anti-missile defence... it will be a big step forward,"* It appears that the Prime Minister did indeed have one foot firmly planted in the old ways. If it was the intention that Medvedev merely keep the presidential chair warm, the arrival on the scene of Barack Obama may have changed everything.

Boris Nikolayevich Yeltsin (1931-2007)
First President of the Russian Federation

appendix 1
vladimir putin

Vladimir Vladimirovich Putin was born on October 7th 1952 in Leningrad (now St Petersburg). His father, Vladimir Spiridonovich Putin (1911–99) was a keen communist, and a member of his factory's party bureau. A former submariner, he had served with the NKVD, forerunner of the KGB, during the Second World War. Although his father was an atheist, in accordance with Marxist doctrine, his mother, Maria Ivanova Shelomova (1911–98) was a devoted Christian, and Putin is said to have been secretly christened as a baby.

On graduating from Leningrad State University in 1975, he entered the 401st KGB training school, subsequently working in the 2nd (counter-intelligence) department. He was then moved to the 1st department, where using the cover of a police officer, his duties involved monitoring the activities of foreigners in the city. He was promoted to the 1st Chief Directorate, which was responsible for foreign operations, including the handling of overseas agents, and the gathering of political and technical intelligence.

Between 1985–90 he was stationed in Dresden in East Germany. Recalled after the collapse of that state, he took up a position at Leningrad University, where his job involved monitoring students and identifying potential recruits for the security services. This assignment was short lived, as he resigned from the KGB in August 1991.

During this time, however, he had re-established links with his former professor, Anatoly Sobchak, who was to play an increasingly important part in his future. Sobchak was, by this time Mayor of St Petersburg, and Putin was appointed to the role of head of the Committee for External Relations. He was also appointed to the boards of several companies, and several other political offices in the city administration followed.

On July 25th 1998 Yeltsin appointed Vladimir Putin head of the FSB (successor to the KGB), an office he occupied until August 1999. He also became a permanent member of the Security Council of the Russian Federation on October 1st 1998 and became Secretary of the Council on March 29th 1999. His first major national office came on August 9th 1999, when he was appointed as one of three First Deputy Prime Ministers. The very same day, President Boris Yeltsin appointed him to the post of acting Prime Minister. One week later, the State Duma confirmed his appointment as Prime Minister.

Yeltsin's resignation, in December 1999 saw Putin being named as Acting President. He won the March 2000 Presidential elections, and was inaugurated as the second President of Russia on May 7th. He was re-elected in March 2004 with 71% of the vote. Limited by national law to two terms of office, he was ineligible to stand in the 2008 presidential elections, and on May 8th 2008 was appointed to the office of Prime Minister.

In 1983 Putin married Ludmilla Shkrebneva. The couple have two daughters, Maria (born 1985) and Yekaterina (born 1986).

appendix 2
dmitry medvedev

Dmitry Anatolyevich Medvedev was born in Leningrad on September 14th 1965. His father, Anatoly Afanasevich Medvedev (1926–2004) was a professor at the Leningrad Institute of Technology. His mother is Yulia Veniaminovna Shaposhnikova (1936 -). Not a particularly gifted student in his earlier years, as a young man he enjoyed listening to western rock music.

He went on to study law, graduating from the Law Department of Leningrad State University in 1987, receiving his PhD in private law in 1990. Like Putin, Medvedev studied under Anatoly Sobchak, and played a prominent role in his mayoral election campaign in 1988. In 1990 he worked in Leningrad Municipal Soviet of People's Deputies under the supervision of Putin. From 1991 to 1996 Medvedev worked under Putin again, as a legal expert for the International Relations Committee of the Saint Petersburg Mayor's Office.

Between 1991–99 he also held a junior academic position at his alma mater. He is one of the authors of a book on civil law, published in 3 volumes, and author of *Questions of Russia's National Development* (2007), a university textbook.

In 1999, Putin was to bring Medvedev to Moscow, where he was appointed deputy head of the presidential staff, and in 2000 was Putin's campaign manager.

He has held a number of commercial positions, most prominently, between 2000–01 he was chair of Gazprom's board of directors, then deputy chair from 2001–02, becoming chair again in June 2002.

In November 2005, Medvedev was appointed as First Deputy Prime Minister.

In 2008, with Putin being barred from running for a third term, Medvedev successfully stood for the Presidency, and was inaugurated on May 7th.

He is married to Svetlana Vladimirovna Linnik (born 1965), and the couple have one son, Ilya (born 1996).

index